Sarah

*From an abusive childhood and
the depths of suicidal despair to
a life of hope and freedom*

Sarah Shaw

Sovereign World

Sovereign World Ltd
PO Box 784
Ellel
Lancaster
LA1 9DA
England

ISBN: 978-1-85240-511-3

The publishers aim to produce books which will help to extend and build up the Kingdom of God. We do not necessarily agree with every view expressed by the authors, or with every interpretation of Scripture expressed. We expect readers to make their own judgment in the light of their understanding of God's Word and in an attitude of Christian love and fellowship.

Cover design by Andrew Mark, ThirteenFour Design
Typeset by **documen**, www.documen.co.uk
Printed in The United Kingdom

For my husband, who selflessly loved,
supported and encouraged me
throughout this journey.

Confidentiality

Some names have been changed to protect
my own and my family's identities.

Contents

Heartfelt thanks to …

Peter and Fiona Horrobin for their faithfulness to the vision for Ellel Ministries that God gave to Peter over thirty years ago, for their compassionate hearts for the hurting and their unwavering belief in God as the Healer and Giver of Life.

Special thanks to those who sacrificially gave of themselves, of their time, energy and resources in so many ways, to walk this journey with me: to Fiona, Anna, Karen, Val and Ian, in particular, through whom God graciously ministered to me and without whom I would not have made it.

My sincere gratitude goes to the wider team at Ellel Grange, and indeed at all the Ellel UK centers, who have laid down their own lives to serve God in ministering to the broken and hurting. As they have warmly welcomed and unconditionally accepted me, carried my bags, prepared rooms and served meals, they have powerfully shown me what it means and what a privilege it is to be part of God's family.

Special thanks, too, to Pam and Christine, who have prayerfully supported me in the writing of this book.

Finally, heartfelt thanks to my husband and children for their patience and perseverance, and for believing in me, in the work God was doing and in real freedom, even through very difficult times.

To God be all the glory, honor and praise.

Foreword by
Dr Geoff Searle

There is now a genre of popular writing known as "Abusive Childhood Experience" which is so accepted that often bookshops have shelves labeled accordingly. Should that be what you are looking for, this is the wrong book for you and I advise you to put it back now. This remarkable book is about true recovery of health by a deeply wronged woman, whom I met more than ten years ago. Rarely is this subject written about, and even more uncommonly in Sarah's calm and thoughtful way.

In my clinical life I am plagued by what the man in the street (thinks he) knows about mental illness – that it is either hopeless or an expression of personal weakness and that as a psychiatrist I am either delusionally inept or useless. Actually patients often get better and get on with their lives, but you never hear of it. This is what I seek for my patients and sometimes the search is more in hope than expectation. Certainly this was the case with Sarah, who came to me with a very serious depression combined with collapsing lifelong coping strategies and a very suspicious absence of childhood memories, which all together spelt big trouble and a bad prognosis.

But (and this is a very big but) she also had qualities and supports that many others do not have. This was not by chance. Although (at the time) she couldn't see it, she was clearly a kind, loving and caring individual who could connect to others far more deeply than she could recognize initially.

She had a husband and family who loved her, along with a relationship with God that was to save her through the efforts of her counselors and her church. However, this is not to down-play her own prolonged and courageous efforts to escape from her horrible upbringing which seemed to have crippled and enslaved her. Recovering from abuse is not (as this book makes clear) a sudden magical lifting of a veil by a stunning insight: it is a daily battle to change the way you think, feel and behave when every fiber of your being screams "no," leaving you emotionally drained. Then the next day you get up and do it again.

Every path to recovery is different, partly based on the individual, but also because of the underpinnings of the therapy, which show through. The route Sarah took was long, but as is usual it was a process of starting again from the beginning and progressing through childhood and adolescence supported by trustworthy and loving adults (therapists). Sarah's greatest triumph is her achievement of coping with the separation from her dependency on therapy without falling apart and then re-starting her adult relationship with her husband.

When I started in psychiatry in the early 1980s no one would ever have considered offering therapy to Sarah as it was "impossible," and those who arrived with problems as complex and deep-rooted as hers were simplified into an illness accessible to medication and limited recovery accepted. Treatment has moved on a long way since then with a multiplicity of therapies developed, many of them in a considerable hurry to help, focusing on thoughts and behaviors and consequently unhelpful with more complex and deep-rooted problems related to the relationship between individuals and of an individual with themselves.

The critical part of helping is actually very simple – being a loving and responsible adult, but this is incredibly complex and difficult with an unpredictable, demanding, screaming, chaotic child/adult. The strength of character to bond, heal and then release a patient is not to be understated, especially with the intense and prolonged involvement that Sarah needed to heal.

I am glad to say that it is now feasible to help almost everyone with serious problems such as Sarah, but a recovery as complete as this would be thought miraculous were it not quite clear from her understated account quite how it came about.

Dr Geoff Searle MB.BS.BSc.FRCPsych
November 2009

Foreword by
Fiona Horrobin

Our twenty-year journey, of reaching out to help people with the deepest of needs, has forged within us an unshakeable belief in the ability of the Creator to restore a broken human life. It was a tremendous privilege, although extremely tough at times, to walk with Sarah through her particular journey to the wholeness and normality that she enjoys today – free to live a normal life with her family, free from drugs, clinical care and the need for any other outside source of help and comfort.

God has truly given her back 'the years that the locusts have eaten' and brought redemption beyond human ability and reasoning. Sarah was referred to us for help by her vicar and released by her psychiatrist to come on a healing retreat. Little did we know, on that first encounter, what lay ahead for both Sarah and ourselves as we set out together on her journey to restoration.

Some time earlier Sarah had reached her personal elastic limit and had finally snapped. Psychiatric help and powerful medication had been needed to help save her from herself and her desire to die. Inside, the real Sarah could no longer silence the pain from years of abusive devastation.

Eventually, as we explored her past together, the external appearance of normality gave way to an inner cavern of pain and brokenness, causing her to believe that, for everyone's sake, it would be better if she were eliminated from this life.

She was not your ordinary or, even, more complex, counselee. Her whole life was built on the belief that she was so bad that she had deserved the unimaginable abuse she had suffered.

The challenge for those of us who were her family and counsellors was, how could we reach such an empty, broken and shattered soul? Was it possible that human love, expressed to her from our Christian belief and hearts, could heal and fill her aching void and need?

Explosion

"My pain is me, it is who I am." Sarah eventually exploded. "You cannot get rid of me." "I hate love." "Love hurts." "Love uses you." The explosion gave way to heaving sobs and shaking of her head. The weariness and fatigue of her walk towards healing had set in and eventually Sarah cried out, "You don't understand what's inside me, it's too big for anyone, I need to go back to the hospital." Bewildered by her cry—we sat with Sarah in silence, deep in our individual thoughts and prayers.

Injustice

In the journey towards healing that I and the counseling team had been on with her, I had tapped into what was the deepest and greatest cry of the human heart – to be valued and loved.

What could I say? What could any one of our team say? What words or actions could be the answer? Sarah had suffered a lifetime of imprisonment for something she had no power to change and something she wasn't guilty of. Would punishment for her abusers be the answer? We had talked and discussed this at length. From the depth of Sarah's soul came the desire for vengeance, yet nothing would be enough to satisfy the injustice – imprisonment or even the death penalty was not enough. It would make her feel better, but only momentarily. It would never satisfy the raging injustice within.

I sat in silence deep in my own thoughts and prayers. Had I gone too far? Sarah had now experienced human love and she was clinging to it at one extreme, but was also fighting it at the other extreme. We had allowed her to taste of something she had never given herself permission to receive. The excruciating truth was that this love was still not enough.

In my private thoughts, I began to think there was no answer and perhaps we had to help her to somehow live with and manage the pain. I even began to doubt whether it truly was possible to see the power of love triumph over such hatred and evil. Maybe we should compromise and settle for at least some partial healing. Yet at a deeper place within me, there would rise up this unshakable conviction that where no human being could change and heal the human heart, the living God could.

The Road to Victory

Sarah's story now stands as a dynamic testimony to the fact that God can and does heal. There is no doubting that without the plumbline of God's Living Word practically applied and lived out, we would not have been able to help Sarah in the way we did. Undeniably, there was something beyond and above our own human effort and gifting at work in Sarah's life.

This something was a relationship – and one which she steadfastly clung to in the person of Jesus Christ. As Scripture was unveiled and applied, there were times without number that gems of essential truth fell from its pages. Scripture came alive with directions of hope, love and purpose. Most crucially it led the way to Sarah's freedom.

God the Creator made us for one purpose – that was for relationship. He made us and created us for love. This was His design. In this perfect design we were given the greatest gift of all – free will – the freedom to think our own thoughts, have our own opinions, to feel our own emotions, painful and joyful, and be our own person. This Creator called us His children, sons and daughters and gave us an inheritance of His love, the knowledge of sins forgiven and eternal life.

Sarah was being carried by God on a journey, which would eventually break down every barrier of hatred and evil, so that she could receive her promised inheritance. For us, as we journeyed with her, with our own faith and trust in a faithful God, who is true to His Word, we received the strength and grace to walk with her through many twists and turns along the road, finding pearls of wisdom and wonderful keys for the inner healing of a human soul, previously destroyed by cruelty and injustice.

Hatred had worked its evil deeds in her life, but love triumphed. This love was Divine, the love of the Creator for His creation, the Father for His child. He rescued her and restored her, and in doing so profoundly changed and touched us too.

As her counselors, we had to dig deep into God also, to find the grace to keep going, in the face of seeming impossibilities. This grace welled up from within us. Nobody on our team can pretend it was an easy walk. There were challenges which took us to the brink of giving up on many occasions. They went beyond the limits of human endurance. Yet, it was at those times that spiritual insights and breakthroughs came and with this the joy and encouragement to press on.

We pray that through the many keys and understandings we received, and through Sarah's faith, courage and determination, others will receive their freedom too. Our thanksgiving goes primarily to God, whose love, and power to heal and save from the worst of abuses, remains our motivation.

We also want to thank all our team, whose sacrificial giving of themselves enabled Sarah to receive the help she needed. Our deepest admiration goes to her husband, John, who was steadfast and loyal throughout the journey and whose integrity is a shining example.

For all of us who have touched Sarah's life, we are richer for it. What the enemy intended for harm, the Lord has turned to good!

Fiona Horrobin
November 2009

Preface

During my childhood I was severely abused by my own parents over many years. There was nowhere to go for comfort, so I grew up burying all the bad times inside myself and blocking them out. I was a child and thought like a child, with no idea of the consequences. All I knew was: I was bad, and when it hurt it was because I deserved it.

For most of my life I didn't understand that my traumatic upbringing had resulted in my personality being fragmented or splintered into eight separate parts. I was suffering from what the handbook used by psychiatrists and psychologists to diagnose mental disorders[1] calls Dissociative Identity Disorder.

But I didn't question the way my life was. I didn't question my extremely irrational beliefs, my obsessive compulsive nature, the constant checking and re-checking, the many fears I tiptoed round, or even the fact that I had no memories of the first eighteen years of my life. I just saw all these things as part of my make-up. They were embarrassing inadequacies I tried to hide.

It wasn't until my mid-thirties that my past really caught up with me. The feelings of guilt that had always nagged away inside began to grow. They were eating me up. I felt guilty for being a bad wife, a bad mother, a bad Christian, a bad friend... In the end I blamed myself for everything. I thought I was "such a bad, bad person" that I even felt guilty for being alive. The self-hatred that flooded up from deep inside, soaked into every fiber of my being until self-loathing hung like dense fog all round me, and I was adamant that I deserved to die.

17

After a serious suicide attempt, I was admitted to a psychiatric hospital, where I was diagnosed with bulimia, Obsessive Compulsive Disorder, severe clinical depression, self-harming and suicidal tendencies. I felt as if I had fallen in slow motion down to the bottom of a deep, dark pit of absolute despair, and I blamed myself.

Like many abused people, I was without hope. Yet, impossible as it seemed to me, there was hope. My vicar and his wife had been trying to help, and along with other friends were praying, and after seven months in hospital the opportunity opened up for me to receive professional Christian help. It was through that help, at a time when I was desperately suicidal, that God gave me a picture of a rose. It was a rose that had been smashed. The petals were crushed and torn, and strewn all over the ground. God said He was going to carefully pick up each petal and lovingly restore it to wholeness.

It was a beautiful picture, but I was in such a mess I couldn't begin to understand how He could do that. But this book is a testimony of His faithfulness to that word and the story of how He has painstakingly rebuilt my life.

As I began to walk free of the chains that held me from my past, I had an appointment with my psychiatrist, along with Fiona, the lead person in the team that had been counseling me. The psychiatrist with his professional expertise confirmed the healing he saw before his eyes, not yet complete but indisputable. I knew I was incredibly privileged to be receiving such solid Christian help, through which God was working powerfully. But I remembered the other patients I had got to know well in hospital, many of whom were desperate, and I thought about the many more I didn't know. I asked him, "What happens to people like me who don't get the help I've received?" I won't forget his reply: "I have a lady just like you at the moment, and I have to face the fact she may not live."

That's the reason I have written this book. It's not an account of the horrors of my upbringing, but a biography of my journey to healing. Many people never recover from abuse, but my prayer is that it will encourage others who are left suffering with the consequences of shocking childhood experiences, that there is a real way out of an abusive past.

So many abused, hurting people don't understand their brokenness. They are stuck, as I was, in the tormenting outworked symptoms of guilt and self-hatred, multiple fears, depression, Obsessive Compulsive Disorder, eating disorders, and even self-harming and suicidal tendencies. They are kept alive – or not – with mind-altering medication that treats the symptoms that seem to be the problem. But the bigger problem is what's not seen, what's been blocked off and buried as dead in the subconscious, yet is not dead but alive and desperate, and needs more than medication.

I know beyond all doubt that real healing can only come through entering humbly and honestly into true and living relationship with our Father God through Jesus. It is the only way to wholeness, freedom from inner conflict and knowing the true security we all long for on the inside – security that brings release from all the devastating symptoms.

Some would say I always had a relationship with God since the time I became a Christian, long before I broke down and was admitted to a psychiatric hospital. But it was a superficial relationship. I understand now that God could only go as far as I allowed Him. And I had blocked off the traumatized places inside, where all the pain, fear, anger and sense of injustice from the cruelty and abuse of my childhood were buried. It was as if I had poured concrete on top and posted big "No Entry" signs in front of them. I learned that I had to let go of all that protection and allow God into the mess, if I was to experience the real freedom He has on His heart for every one of us.

I want to share something of my struggle to do that, in a very real way, but also in a way that imparts real hope in the living God, who can gather up the petals of a broken life and restore them to wholeness.

Jesus said,

> "You will know the truth and the truth will set you free."
>
> (John 8:32)

He also proclaims that He has come to fulfill God's words spoken through the prophet Isaiah:

> "He has sent me to bind up the broken-hearted, to proclaim freedom for the captives, and release from darkness for the prisoners."
>
> (Isaiah 61:1; see also Luke 4:18-21)

To Him, be all the praise, all the glory and all the honor.

Note

1. Diagnostic and Statistical Manual of Mental Disorders, fourth edition text revision or DSM-IV-TR.

CHAPTER 1

When Can I Go Home?

At thirty-six, I had a good marriage, and John and I had two lovely children. Tom was eleven and in his first year at Grammar School, and Beth was nine and a year ahead of her peers at school. I had become a Christian through attending infant baptism classes when Tom was born, and was working part-time as the Parish Secretary.

From the outside everything looked so normal. Perhaps at that time in many ways things *were* normal, maybe even better than normal. There is no doubt a lot of good has come into my life and I have much to be thankful for.

Hiding Abuse

But I had formed a lifetime's habit of making things look normal even when they weren't. It was more of a lifestyle than a habit, which began when very bad things happened in my childhood.

Between the ages of three and eighteen my father repeatedly sexually abused me. And on every occasion, immediately after he'd finished and pushed me aside and left the room, I rushed to wash and dress, and straighten bedclothes, rugs and anything else that had been disturbed. I was afraid of my mother knowing what had been going on.

Despite my best efforts, she always knew. And there were many times when I was shut in my room for days and nights at a time "in disgrace, to think about how bad I was." When I was released she sent me back to school with a sick note offering an excuse for my absence, and I behaved as if nothing had happened. Whatever the cost, everything had to look normal. That was how my mother was, and that was how I grew up.

The Parish Office was a busy place with people calling in with messages for the clergy, to enquire about services, meetings and rotas, and to arrange weddings, funerals and baptisms. I smiled and worked hard to please everyone, offering to do their typing and photocopying, and anything else I could to help.

I was the helpful, friendly Parish Secretary, the efficient wife who kept the house and garden immaculate, and the mother who ferried the children to as many activities as we could fit into a week, and offered to take other people's children as well. At least this was who I was on the outside.

Inside was different. Inside I was insecure and struggling with a cast-iron certainty that I was a very bad person. I was increasingly weighed down with guilt and a deep sense of hopelessness. It's true that victims of abuse often take onto themselves the guilt that belongs to their abuser, but I had no memory, nor indeed any idea, that I had been abused, and nor did John. I just felt "bad."

In reality, I hadn't just tried to hide the abuse under a blanket of pretense. I had completely lost the memory of the first eighteen years of my life, and unwittingly created a different past for myself. "I was a difficult child," I would tell people, firmly believing what I was saying. "I gave my parents a hard time, but they were good and did their very best for me." It felt like the truth to me but it wasn't the truth.

Survival Instinct

The truth was that breaking away from the horrors of my past and blocking out those years had been an automatic response. It was basic human survival instinct at work. When comfort is withheld and cruel punishment unleashed on a child whose innocence has been violated by his or her own parents, the pain and injustice are far too great for that child to carry. And that was how I "lost my memory."

Self-hatred and Depression

As an adult, I couldn't explain my deepening depression, except through the belief that I was born bad. And that drove me to try harder at everything I did, to compensate somehow. But it didn't work. I still felt bad. I secretly controlled my eating, took over a hundred laxatives a week, and regularly made myself sick. But I still felt fat. And I felt guilty because I thought Christians were supposed to be happy inside as well as outside.

If I wasn't focused and busy, the bad feelings pushed to the fore, and I just wanted to give up and die. Eventually I went to my doctor, who prescribed anti-depressants and, later, tranquilizers and sleeping tablets. But they didn't control the negative feelings, which became harder and harder to escape until, ultimately, they began to overwhelm me. I became convinced that I was not just a bad person, but a bad Christian, a bad friend, a bad wife and a bad mother. I was like a stick of rock with the word "bad" written all the way through the center.

My faith taught me that no matter how bad we are, Jesus has taken our punishment and won eternal life for everyone who receives Him as their Savior. But I couldn't receive His forgiveness and I couldn't grasp that I could go to heaven. The best I could do was to picture myself curled up and hiding behind everyone else in heaven, afraid of being seen. In the end I couldn't even believe that. I thought I was the exception and didn't just deserve to die when the time came, but deserved to be cut off from life there and then.

Although my sense of worthlessness and self-loathing was extreme enough to make me suicidal, I didn't live in the intensity of it all the time. I would automatically flip out of it when I was at work or with other people, defaulting to that person who tried so hard to please everyone.

It was as if I put on a mask without realizing it, so that I didn't just fool other people, I fooled myself too. When I wasn't consumed with suicidal feelings, I couldn't connect to them at all. It was more than a mood swing, more like a constant switching between one extreme personality and another.

John and one or two close friends saw the changes. They knew I carried razor blades around in my handbag ready to punish myself when I was desperate, and they knew I could switch at any moment. There would be a trigger: perhaps if I hadn't managed to complete every last job at the office, or deadhead every flower in the garden. Or perhaps if I felt I'd been rejected. All these things were like lightning conductors that instantly drew the bitter, self-destructive thoughts and feelings to the surface.

I had confided in my vicar and his wife and they were counseling me. One day when I called at the vicarage to keep an appointment, Barbara told me apologetically that Geoff had been called away. I smiled and said, reassuringly, "That's OK. I understand." We chatted and had a cup of tea together. I went home and swallowed the contents of a bottle of paracetamol.

Although I was very sick, I made John promise not to call a doctor. After a few days I went back to work as if nothing had happened, unaware that my liver was severely damaged.

It was a confusing time, particularly for John. I went from being desperately suicidal one minute to accusing myself of being attention-seeking and believing there was nothing wrong with me the next.

Psychiatric Hospital

Following the next check-up with my doctor, a psychiatrist called Dr Searle was asked to make an assessment. He came the next day and, to my shock, contacted the psychiatric hospital from my home to arrange for a bed to be made available. "I'm admitting you," he said, "because you are a danger to yourself."

My medical notes contain the letter Dr Searle wrote to my GP following this home visit, in which he states:

> *In her mental state, I found Sarah to be a thin, rather anxious woman ... she was obviously depressed. My impression is that she is suffering from a severe depressive illness predicated upon emotionally abusive upbringing ... I think she requires effective anti-depressant treatment ... I expect that her psychological difficulties will need more than a simple intervention from your counselor ...*

John and the children took me to the hospital that evening. We waited in a scruffy room where the paint was peeling off the walls and the carpet curling up at the edges. We could smell cigarette smoke wafting in from outside. None of us had ever set foot in a psychiatric hospital before. It felt dirty, although it probably wasn't. We didn't say very much. I felt guilty, and they were worried. The sound of the occasional patient shuffling past the doorway broke into our thoughts. We all looked up but none of the patients turned to look at us. They stared lifelessly down at the floor, dragging their feet as they made their way up and down the corridor.

After two hours the duty psychiatrist, who had been tied up on an emergency, came to admit me. We answered his questions and signed the necessary forms, and I said "Bye-bye" to my family. The children were fighting back tears, but John chivvied them along. "Come on," he said. "Let's go home. Mum needs to go to bed now. We'll come and see her again tomorrow."

But inside he was more distressed than they were. At home he sat up until the early hours, struggling to come to terms with having left me at such a place.

As I began to put my things in the locker next to a bed in a ward where there were seven other beds, one of the other patients came over and whispered, "Make sure you lock that locker." She nodded at the woman in the bed next to mine. "She's a thief. She'll take your things if you don't lock it."

I was stunned to find myself in this place that was so alien to me. "When can I go home?" I mumbled to the nurse as I reached the front of the queue of patients, waiting to be given our medication. "You'll see Dr Searle on Friday," she said. "You can ask him then." I held out my hand to take the tablets from her. "No," she said impatiently, as I turned to walk away, "put them in your mouth. I want to see you swallow them." I did as she said.

The next morning I felt as if there was nothing wrong with me, and couldn't believe I needed to be in hospital. I was angry that I'd taken the overdose, and angry that I'd told Dr Searle about it. I felt stupid and guilty, and tried to get away from the feelings by talking to the other patients about their problems. I listened and tried to find encouraging and comforting words to help them. Seeking to be the answer to their struggles helped me forget about my own.

I had gone into hospital on a Wednesday, and was sure I would be home by the weekend. I began to feel embarrassed at the prospect of seeing Dr Searle. I was worried that he would say I was there under false pretenses and wasting National Health resources. Friday felt like a long time to wait.

When a nurse eventually called me in to see him, I was taken aback that he asked so many questions, especially about my childhood. I thought he was on the wrong track completely and wasting his time. I could never remember things about my past, and anyway I didn't believe it had anything to do with the reason I was in hospital.

When he asked about how things were with my parents now, I was honest about my difficult relationship with my mother. And I told him apologetically that I was quite fearful of my father, explaining that he was a big, loud, forceful man and most people were uncomfortable around him. I was sure none of this was relevant.

When he finally asked why I had overdosed, I felt he had got to the real issue. I told him that it was because I was angry with myself for not trying harder in life, for being a failure, for the anxiety and stress I had brought on John and the children, for letting them all down so badly, for being such a bad person. I told him I hated myself. But even after admitting all this, I didn't think I needed to be in hospital. I thought he was going to discharge me.

At the end of the interview, I asked, "When can I go home?" It was mid-September, and he said firmly, "With a fair wind, you could be out by Christmas." I was stunned. I shook his hand mechanically and walked down the corridor, his words ringing in my ears. How could that be right?

Flashbacks

Dr Searle arranged regular appointments with a psychologist, Wendy, who said I had kept obsessively busy and focused on outward things all my life, to suppress my negative emotions from the past, which were now surfacing in the present. What she said made sense, but there was nothing I knew of, or could connect to, from my past that could account for the way I felt in the present.

I couldn't get away from the belief that I was born bad, and the conviction that I had tried as hard as I could to change myself, but had failed. I hated myself and I wanted to die. It wasn't complicated to me, there wasn't anything else to it, and it didn't have anything to do with my upbringing.

But there was a picture that repeatedly came into my mind, usually at night. I would wake up, hot and frightened,

thinking it was real. It was a picture of me as a child standing naked, with my father looking at me. I hated it and tried
to push it away and shut it out of my head. Wendy encouraged me to talk about it. I was reluctant and shook my head
violently afterwards to shake it away. I didn't understand it
and I didn't want to make it mean something it didn't.

Concerned Friends

I had a lot of visitors especially people from my church. They
were shocked when they heard where I was, because I had
been "such a happy person" and pleased everyone so well. But
in reality, even though I wasn't yet facing it myself, inside I was
a mess and completely broken down.

I felt I owed everyone an explanation. I couldn't stop
working out people's expectations and trying to fulfill them. I
wanted each person to feel they had a worthwhile visit. Afterwards, I went over and over the conversations, and beat myself
up both mentally and physically for not saying the right things.
I would dig my fingernails into my wrists until they bled, and
punch my legs until eventually they were permanently shades
of purple, black and blue.

My most violent attack on myself was after a visit from my
father. A concerned nurse came to my rescue. I just kept telling her over and over again that I was bad. She gave me some
tranquilizers and said she would ask John to ask my father not
to visit anymore, at least for a while.

My Parents' Responses

My father was a strong, heavy man with a quick temper, which
everyone has always tiptoed round. His second wife lived on
her nerves, constantly trying to pre-empt his violent explo-
sions. And I knew he had served several prison sentences for
violence and theft, one of them during the time of my birth.

John was understandably anxious about telling him he wasn't allowed to visit me anymore. He met him in the hospital car park and, sitting in the car together, told him there was a possibility that I had been abused as a child. He said the hospital had asked that he should stop visiting for the time being. John was shocked to see the blood rush to my father's face as he listened silently. Then, without saying a word, he got out of the car and walked away. We never saw him again.

Other people were asked to curtail their visits too, and although I felt guilty, it was a relief to get away from putting on a performance. In the end, overriding the reality of how I felt inside had become too much and, together with the sedating effect of the medication, had brought me to exhaustion point.

There was only one person I wanted to see, and I ached for her to come. It was my mum. She had long been divorced from my father, and I wanted to see her more than anything. I was desperate for her to show me that she cared.

As far back as I could remember, I had waited for an expression of her love, and had made countless excuses for her, and blamed myself completely when she let me down. In the waiting I had looked for substitutes. When I left school it was the manager of the store where I worked. Then when I became a manager it was the area manager. Then my vicar's wife. And there in the hospital it was my key nurse. Without even realizing I was doing it, I had befriended and got alongside a whole string of women and tried, sometimes successfully, to manipulate each one to mother me. But the need had never been met.

Having landed up as a patient in a locked ward of a psychiatric hospital, I felt as if I had hit rock bottom. I was depressed and ashamed. And the longing for my mother's love at times was overpowering. I would become like a child, sobbing and repeating over and over again, "I want my mum." Just like a child, I felt that if my mother would just come and hold me in her arms, everything would be all right.

My mother was also John's secretary. That was how I had met him. He had given her a lift home on a rainy day, and we began to see one another. At first she didn't seem to mind, but as we grew close and eventually began to talk about marriage, she turned against him. John's relationship with my mother went from being a good working relationship to the most strained and difficult relationship he had ever experienced, either before or since. She would only relate with him on a strictly work basis, and when we eventually married she burnt every childhood photograph of me and would have nothing at all to do with us on a personal, family level.

We had tried repeatedly to resolve the difficulties but it always ended in impasse. It was no different when I was in hospital. The psychologist contacted her to ask her to visit, but she refused.

The Psychiatric Diagnosis

Ultimately, the psychiatric team working with me diagnosed severe clinical depression, bulimia, Obsessive Compulsive Disorder, and self-harming and suicidal tendencies.

My medical notes, written not by Dr Searle but by another Consultant Psychiatrist at the hospital (Dr Franklin), state:

> *This is not a straightforward case … The evidence is that Sarah's depression has elements in it of both a major illness (Endogenous Depression) and an understandable reaction to stress (Reactive Depression). It is possible, some would say probable, that the second element represents a delayed consequence of early sexual abuse.*

This is the diagrammatical analysis of the root causes of those outworked conditions, drawn at the time by the key nurse who was assigned to me:

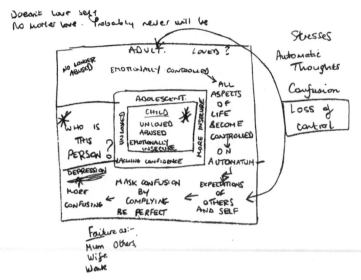

Figure 1.

It was true that I was depressed and full of self-hatred, and my heart cry was, "Who am I?", but with no memory of abuse or neglect in childhood, I could not embrace the psychiatric diagnosis. Even though there were difficulties with both my parents, and things had come up in hospital that seemed to confirm what the team were saying, I thought they'd got it wrong. I continued to believe that I had been a very bad child, and that my parents were essentially good people who had done their best with me.

Denial Reinforced

I had no understanding whatsoever at that time that the abuse of my childhood was so severe and painful that I had separated (or disassociated) from the entire first eighteen years of my life.

I had developed all sorts of complicated ways of maintaining denial. My mind, with its strong powers of reasoning, had become so highly tuned that it was like a fortress around the truth of my past. The false beliefs, like the lie that I was bad, had become truth to me. And I used circumstances all the time to "prove" what I believed was truth. When my mother didn't visit me in hospital, it *proved* to me that I was bad and I didn't deserve a visit from her. And I cut my wrists to punish myself for wanting her love.

The psychiatric team worked hard to try to relieve my symptoms, prescribing varying dosages and combinations of different types of medication, and encouraging me in whatever ways they could. It wasn't easy for them, because the guilt that festered inside was always looking for something to anchor itself to. And I habitually filtered out all the good things that were spoken to me, and dwelt on any negative word I could find, using it to beat myself up.

But they didn't give up and I am deeply grateful. I have been incredibly blessed to have people around me through-out my journey who have always cared, even when I couldn't receive the help they were offering. I thank God in particular for the medics, who kept me alive during that time.

As the weeks and months went by, I withdrew more and more inside myself. I felt as if I was in a dark tunnel and I couldn't see the end. The only way to go was to keep taking the medication and to take advantage of the opportunities I was given to talk to the psychiatrist and psychologist.

Although I was a Christian, I didn't find comfort in read-ing the Bible. I used it like everything else – to beat myself up. I would dwell on a verse I knew, like, "This is the day the Lord has made; let us rejoice and be glad in it" (Psalm 118:24), and then try to be positive and joyful, but I couldn't rise above the sense of hopelessness that was so real to me and the desire to just give up on life. And when my efforts to be a "good, joyful" Christian ended in defeat, I hated and punished myself all the more.

There was no yielding of the deeply entrenched, irrational thoughts and beliefs, and I stubbornly held on to my escape

plan: "There's a way out of all this. I can take my own life."
Yet, somehow, even at my worst times there was always a fight
in me. And I fought to resist that escape route.

John's Struggle

In January 1996, John was relieved to be invited to a meeting
at the hospital to discuss my treatment. For a long time he had
been asking the hospital staff the same question, "What's the
answer for my wife?"

The psychiatric team went through my case notes, dis-
cussing the different types of medication they had tried, and
looked at what had been covered with the psychologist. The
last resort was electric shock treatment, but I was refusing this.
Eventually, in frustration John looked at Dr Searle and asked,
"Where do we go from here?" Unable to give him an answer,
the psychiatrist shrugged his shoulders and threw his hands up
in the air.

There didn't seem to be a way forward, and John felt he
was coming to the end of his own limitations. He was grieving
the loss of his father, who had been living with us for ten years
and had died of lung cancer while I was in hospital. He was
also going through an extremely stressful time at work, having
been left to carry the load when the managing director walked
out of the business. My mother was working as his secretary
but refusing to enter into any kind of personal conversation,
let alone offer any help or support. And he was single-hand-
edly trying to care for our two children.

He struggled to come to terms with my extreme mental
state and the reasons for it that seemed to be coming to light. It
was hard for him to reconcile in his own mind, even with what
he knew of my mother and his suspicions of my father, that I
was so depressed and needed such high dosages of psychiatric
medication, and might yet be given electric shock treatment.
And he was troubled by the sight and sound of all the keys the

staff jangled as they locked and unlocked doors behind him when he came to visit. It was a world that neither of us had ever experienced before.

I had been a person who was always in control of life with a successful career as a manager in the retail business behind me. Yet I had reached a place where I had been put on a lifetime's incapacity benefit, and even the Consultant Psychiatrist was now at a loss to know how to help.

A Door of Hope

Dr Searle's best suggestion was electric shock treatment, but he couldn't tell us how it worked. I didn't want to have it, not least because our Team Rector, David, who had taken over pastoral care for me from Geoff and had been visiting with his wife, Caroline, said he didn't think it was a good idea. In those days, I was afraid of God, but it wasn't so much a reverent fear as a fear of His disappointment in me and the punishment He might unleash on me if I didn't do what He said I should do.

Because there wasn't any other treatment the hospital could offer, the staff began to try to persuade me to consent to ECT. Just as I was on the brink of relenting, David came and told me that he had contacted Ellel Grange, a Christian Healing Center in the north of England, to ask if there was any help available for me there.

I was invited to attend a ten-day Healing Retreat. The hospital agreed to release me to go on two conditions. The first was that I must have a carer with me. And the second was that if I didn't come back with a significant sign of improvement, I would be sectioned and forced to undergo ECT.

CHAPTER 2

I Hate Love!

When I arrived at Ellel Grange on 28 February 1996, I had been a psychiatric patient for five months. I had many fears, the worst of which was a deep fear of people, especially people I knew. I was afraid of what they might think of me. It felt as if the word "Nutcase" was written across my forehead for everyone to see and I was so ashamed I had completely withdrawn inside myself.

On visits home from hospital, I stayed indoors afraid to step outside even to hang the washing on the line. I insisted that John park the car in the garage so that people would think we were out. And when the doorbell did ring, in panic I would run to a place where I could crouch down behind an armchair or a bed, so that I couldn't be seen through any windows.

There were a few occasions when John persuaded me to go to the shops, in attempts to draw me out of isolation and into normal life, but I never made it to the checkout. Testing his patience to the limit, I would leave him stranded in the middle of an aisle with goods to pay for, as I ran back to the safety of the car.

Over the last twelve years Ellel Grange has become a very special place to me. However, as Caroline, the Rector's wife, drove the car up the long driveway on that first visit, I completely missed the beauty and peace that characterize Ellel Grange. I was oblivious of the stunning grounds all around, and when we stepped inside the huge doors, even the grandeur of the beautiful sweeping staircase in the entrance hall escaped my attention.

I hid behind Caroline as she dealt with the business of signing in at reception, anxious to get away from the people who were milling about, waiting for the planned program to begin. I was intent on retreating to the safety of the bedroom.

For most of the ten days I kept my head bowed, as if in some childlike way I thought that if I didn't see other people they might not see me. I shuffled my feet and kept my sleeves pulled well down to hide the scars on my wrists.

A Faulty Foundation

On the first evening I was introduced to the people who were going to counsel me during my visit. Their names were Fiona, Paul and Ann. They immediately looked like very good and kind people. All the worst I thought about myself surged to the fore. "They're good and I'm bad. They're good Christians. They'll be shocked at what a rubbish Christian I am ... Am I a Christian? ... I'm probably not ... I shouldn't be here ... I'm so bad ..." Panic rose up with the fear of the unknown. What would these good and godly people ask and expect of me?

The reality was, I didn't know either what they might expect of me or what I should expect of them. I had thought that perhaps I would be prayed for in the same way as I had been in the past. It was around the time of the Toronto Blessing,[1] and before breaking down completely and going into hospital, I had attended weekly Toronto-style "Times of Refreshing" meetings held in our church. I remember shaking, falling on the floor and manifesting as many others did. I was grateful that people were willing to pray for me, but sadly I didn't experience any long-term benefit.

The psychiatric team's main focus had been on outward symptoms, with medication prescribed to control them and regular therapy sessions looking at how I could work at changing my thoughts and behavior. Because I was bulimic and underweight, much of my care plan was centered on eating. But it just became a fight against the nurses, to try and get away with eating as little as possible and to get rid of whatever I did eat. Twice-weekly weigh-ins fuelled my obsession that I was fat, which in turn fuelled my self-loathing.

At Ellel Grange the approach was completely different. No one asked about my symptoms or medical diagnosis. No one seemed to notice whether I ate the dinner or not, and whether I went to the bathroom to get rid of it afterwards or not.

The focus was entirely on spiritual truth and how it outworks in our lives. There were teaching sessions in a large ornate meeting room, which all the counselees attended. We sat in rows of chairs with our counselors alongside, as the teachers talked sensitively about how God made each one of us for relationship – to love and be loved, but if our parents hadn't affirmed and cherished us as children, protected us, and given us right boundaries and the safety to fail and not be punished, we were like plants that hadn't been adequately fed and watered. We never came into our full potential and blossomed in life, but instead grew up with fears and insecurities, feelings of worthlessness and, perhaps, even self-hatred.

Until that time, I had only looked at my mental illness from an outward perspective, at the ways it affected me, and others. I couldn't or wouldn't embrace a root cause of childhood abuse, because it felt like an excuse to blame someone else for the way I was. I couldn't let myself off the hook because, in my eyes, I was the guilty one.

The teaching I heard at Ellel Grange was gentle but profound. It gave me a new perspective and enabled me to begin to look deeper. It helped me to understand that my life, like many other people's, probably wasn't built on a good foundation of love and truth, and because of that I didn't see myself as precious and valuable, which is how the Bible says God sees me.

And I didn't see God and His love for me as it really is either. I didn't see it as generous and unconditional, but as somehow dismissive, disapproving, harsh and punishing whenever I "got it wrong," which in my book was all the time. I thought God's "good love" was for others, not me.

I began to see that it was as if I was wearing a pair of glasses that gave a distorted view. One of the teachers described it as having a pile of jigsaw pieces that I had tried to make into a picture, but there were some pieces missing and some pieces that belonged to a different puzzle.

Over those ten days, I realized that I needed to measure the things I thought and believed against something that gave a straight edge of truth, and that was the Bible. I had never understood before that the Bible could be so practical and relevant. There were things I didn't like in it – I didn't like it that it said I was forgiven, because I believed and felt I was so guilty and deserved to be punished. But knowing in my heart that the Bible is God's Word, and as such an absolute, I began to see that it had the potential to somehow give me a foothold on which to build my life, even though it wasn't going to be easy to take on board what it said. A glimmer of hope stirred in me, something I had never had before.

The key verse for the ten-day Healing Retreat was Zephaniah 3:17, and one of the musicians at the center wrote a song based on that verse, which everyone sang together. The first line was, "The Lord your God delights in you, and in His love will give you new life." I certainly didn't want the life I was living, which was like a living death. I wanted that new life, but it was very hard to believe that God really did have it for me, and even harder to believe He delighted in me.

The Legacy of My Past

Some people would say I just needed to exchange the lies I believed for truth. But simply exchanging "I'm bad" with "God says, 'I'm good'" wouldn't have dealt with the legacy of having lived with that belief ever since I could remember. My life was formed and shaped around it.

Although at one level, I didn't appear to have any problems until just before I went into hospital, the reality was that I had multiple inner problems and complex personality disorders. I had never had any memory of my first eighteen years, and had spent my whole life striving to make everything look good on the outside to keep hidden, mostly from myself, what I believed was bad on the inside.

Striving was tied up with the treadmill of perfectionism that always demands more and is never satisfied. And the lifestyle of perfectionism had become increasingly ritualistic and obsessive in every area of my life.

I made meticulously detailed lists of everything I thought I should achieve each day and painstakingly crossed the jobs off when they were completed but, as Dr Searle had observed, I always set myself up to fail. The lists were too long and ever increasing in length. It simply became a no-win situation: it didn't matter how hard I worked I could never achieve all that I demanded of myself, and this always led to a deep sense of failure and self-recrimination, and then further resolve to achieve more.

Right up until the evening I went into hospital, everything in our house was permanently, regimentally lined up: ornaments on the mantelpiece, fringes on the rugs, towels on the towel rail, and crockery and tins of food in the cupboards. Recipes had to be followed to the precise letter. And I was the same in the garden: flowerpots in the greenhouse stood like soldiers on parade, and flowerbeds were planted in perfectly straight lines, with carefully measured equidistant gaps in between.

When Tom and Beth were born, I had no concept of bonding and relating with them. I just listed from childcare textbooks the jobs babies generate and worked hard at them. I kept the children and everything around them neat and in its place. When they were playing I constantly tidied their toys behind them, and when they were asleep, I got up in the night to straighten their duvets.

And I had brought all that striving into my Christian life as well, which was sadly not much more than a list of jobs to be mercilessly worked at. I read my Bible, prayed mechanically through lists of prayer items and attended meetings. I couldn't just let go and receive the forgiveness and freedom Jesus had won for me. I didn't know how to let go and "lean into God's grace." That was just jargon to me. I didn't understand what it meant. No, I wanted law – rules and regulations to follow and to work at. I wouldn't have known who I was without the cycle of striving, missing the mark, feeling guilty and punishing myself, and striving harder.

In my desperation to find some solidity, some sense of security inside, Obsessive Compulsive Disorder (OCD) had spread from one area of my life to the next to the next. It had eventually led to seriously controlling my eating and body weight, starving myself, making myself sick and taking laxatives.

In reality OCD and bulimia were controlling me. I hated the constant worry about food, and the pressure of lists, tidying, straightening, checking and re-checking and never being able to relax. I envied people whose houses felt comfortable and lived in. Yet if everything in my house wasn't in perfect order, and if I wasn't working at getting it all in perfect order, I was terrified that everything would spiral out of control.

Eventually, I had reached the point where I couldn't live with all the self-inflicted pressure anymore, but I couldn't live without it either. Somehow it helped me to keep a grip on life.

The legacy of believing I was bad all my life was like a prison sentence. It had robbed me of spontaneity and joy.

It had made my marriage and relationships with my children mechanical and unfeeling, and life nothing more than a demanding list of jobs to be worked at. In the end it had led to severe depression, self-harming and suicidal tendencies, all of which were utterly devastating for John and the children.

The Beginning of a Journey

My life felt like a big mess, like a tangled-up ball of wool, and I didn't even know where the end of the wool was, to begin to untangle it.

Mercifully, God knew, and He had a plan to lead me one step at a time, if I was willing to walk with Him and the servant-hearted team at Ellel Grange He was asking to support me.

If I had known then that this journey to healing was going to take ten years, I don't think I would have gone back to Ellel Grange again. From a logistical viewpoint, the center is three hundred miles from my home and the hospital, in the south of England. And the thought of ten years of battling with painful emotional issues would have been a daunting prospect, not just for me but for John and the Ellel Grange team as well. But I am able to say now with a grateful heart that I am so glad that God's ways are not our ways.

Even though I desperately wanted a copy of God's agenda, so that I could make my own assessment of it and work hard to somehow make it happen, He didn't give me one! He only revealed what He was working on at any one particular time. He didn't shine a light into the future and show me the path ahead.

I have often thought the journey God has taken me on has been like a mountain expedition. I couldn't scale the higher slopes, even with Him as my Guide, until I had been prepared on the lower slopes. I needed to learn about the thing I would have to depend on the most in the tough times ahead: God's immense, unconditional love, in a way I had never known it before.

He worked through John, who never stopped supporting and encouraging me whatever the personal cost, and through Fiona and the Ellel Grange team.

A Model of Jesus and Relationship with Him

The team were willing to listen prayerfully to God on my behalf and spent many hours showing me what He was really like. They patiently heard my heart, encouraged, affirmed, laughed and cried with me, and weren't afraid to confront me lovingly when I needed it. They openly shared their hearts with me, and though I found it virtually impossible to receive, they showed in a myriad of ways that they really cared about my physical, mental, emotional and spiritual wellbeing.

Essentially, during those first ten days at Ellel Grange the team were modeling Jesus, His character and nature, and their relationship with Him to me. Because they all came from solid Christian backgrounds and were mature Christians themselves, they could hold up a straight plumbline of truth, which helped me to see the distortions in my own life.

I saw that they had a real love for Jesus that transcended circumstances. It was a response to Him that came from deep within. They knew Him intimately and heard His voice, and believed unfailingly in His promises. Even though I sat before them at times in the pit of despair, they firmly trusted Him for my healing. They would praise Him for all He had accomplished on the cross and speak out their thankfulness for all He had on His heart for me for that particular day. They banished the works of darkness and ushered in His healing. They had a confidence in Him and a deep sense of peace and joy that wasn't false or transient, that I knew I didn't have.

An Important Milestone

Psalm 42:7 says, "Deep calls to deep," and that was what I experienced. As the team modeled their relationship with Jesus to me, the Spirit of God in the deep places, the spirits of my counselors, was reaching out to the deep place of my spirit in me. And from that place I wanted what I saw they had in their lives.

Although I was desperate to be healed of my fears and obsessions, my eating disorder, depression and self-hatred, to be free of psychiatric labels and medication and able to live a "normal" life with my husband and family, I saw something at Ellel Grange that I wanted even more. I wanted to have that response to Jesus that I saw in these people. I wanted to be so secure in what He did for me on the cross that my only response was to love Him back, by walking with Him in living relationship day by day by day, confident and trusting in Him, no matter what the circumstances.

Reaching this milestone was a key point in my journey because there were many times to come when God would challenge me. I would have to choose whether I wanted to continue with my own way of numbing pain by blocking it out, or yield to His way and face the flashbacks and memories, trusting that He was big enough to carry me through them. He would give me choices too about following Jesus' example in forgiving what seemed unforgivable, and walking out of fears and letting go of false comforts.

They were never easy choices to make. But if the desire hadn't been awakened in me to want relationship with Him more than healing, there wouldn't have been anything for God's Spirit to work with.

Desperation and the Beginning of Hope

It was a tremendous privilege to attend the ten-day Healing Retreat. I learnt so much and found a seed of hope that I had never had before. Yet there was still a very real part of me that wanted to hold fast to controlling everything tightly, particularly my environment and the food that went in and out of my body, and there was still the strong underlying desire to just give up and die.

But I was going back to the hospital with a lot to think about and then, unexpectedly, on the last day Fiona asked me, "If we agree to see you again, are you willing to walk this walk, whatever it takes?" Even though I wasn't prepared for the question, I said, "Yes," for two important reasons.

The first was desperation. I hated the way life was. I knew I was different inside to the way I was on the outside. There were times when I was alone and I would look in the mirror and stare in true confusion at the reflection I hated. With an aggressive tone I would whisper under my breath, "Who are you?" And I couldn't answer the question.

It was as if I had been on the run from myself all my life. I'd had enough, but I didn't know how to stop. I couldn't fix the problem and just be me – I didn't know how to, and the hospital didn't have the keys to help me either. Although full of fear, I was desperate enough to want to allow the lid to be lifted off whatever was hidden inside me, so that I could be transparent, the same on the inside as I was on the outside.

The second reason was that at Ellel Grange I saw that God was holding out to me something even more precious than my healing, and from somewhere deep inside I wanted it.

I returned to the hospital with that small seed of hope, and the psychiatric team were thrilled to see for the first time a positive change in me. Wendy, the psychologist, asked for copies of the audio tapes of the teaching I had heard at Ellel Grange, and later told me that they were profoundly helpful. Dr Searle withdrew his recommendation for electric shock treatment, agreeing to release me to go to Ellel Ministries for further help, with the proviso that a carer accompanied me.

Suddenly a positive way forward was opening up. John and I were both relieved and grateful.

I began regular trips either to Ellel Grange or to one of the other Ellel centers in the south, to see Fiona with another counselor, a different one at each place. To begin with, Caroline also went with me as my carer.

I was transferred from being an in-patient to a day patient at the psychiatric hospital. This meant attending the hospital from nine till five, five days a week, when I was at home, with Dr Searle endorsing the Christian help I was receiving through Ellel Ministries.

The Conflict of Love

At first, I was completely locked into trying to be "good" and please my counselors, just as I had sought to do on the original retreat. I was compliant with everything they asked of me. When they asked me to pray, I prayed. When they asked if I could forgive, I forgave. When they asked if I felt I needed to repent, I repented. When they left to go home in the evening, I freely released them to go.

But through them God, in His mercy, was reaching down into the very core of me. In giving their time and practically exhibiting all the patience, gentleness and kindness of God's love through the way they related, something stirred in me. It was as if the warmth of love was reaching a place deep inside that had been frozen for a long, long time.

This place in me began to thaw and as it did, it came to life with a vengeance. It was a hunger for love that was so intense it frightened me. It correlated exactly with the ravenous feeling I was familiar with when I starved myself and wanted to grab and eat whatever food I could get my hands on. From a deep place within, I suddenly wanted to grab and soak up every touch, every hug, every bit of kindness and gentleness I could get. There was an utter desperation for it.

Yet, at the same time, just as I refused myself food, I had an extremely violent negative response to love. I was suspicious of it and suspicious of its motives. And as time went by, my desire to please and comply took a back seat to the mistrusting, self-protective response to love that God was drawing out into the light. There were many times when the inner turmoil exploded, and it was obvious that the "good" image I had created on the outside really didn't match up to the mess that was on the inside.

I became obnoxious and judgmental and fired strings of angry questions and bitter accusations at the team like bullets from a machine gun: "Why are you being kind? You don't really love me! Why do you want to give me a hug? Is it because it's your job? Is it because God's told you to?" Acts of kindness and love flushed out a revulsion that made me want to reject and hit out at the very people who were throwing a lifeline to me.

Love felt bad. It felt wrong. And it felt wrong to want it, and especially to want it like a child. Although deep down I had wanted love all my life, I had also found excuses all my life for why I shouldn't want it and shouldn't have it: "I'm bad; I'm wicked; I'm dirty; I'm vile; I hate myself; I don't deserve to be loved."

But God was revealing the truth to me that all my efforts to kill the desire for love hadn't killed it at all, but had squashed it down and put it under such pressure that it couldn't be contained for very much longer, and was ready to burst out at any time.

I was ashamed of the intensity of the craving. It felt degrading as an adult to long to be hugged and touched and mothered. I hated it. And because of that, just as I refused physical food, I fought and refused the very love God knew I needed, and was pouring out to me through the team.

When they reached out to hug me, I shrugged them off. When they affirmed me, I didn't believe them. When they offered me something nice to eat, I told them I wasn't hungry, and when they gave me presents, I gave them back. I was actively fighting to try and make Fiona and the rest of the team reject me.

It was as if a civil war was raging inside. I ached for love, yet there were deeply held convictions holding me back from receiving it, convictions that said:

– Love is bad

– To want love is bad

– You can't trust love

– Love will hurt you

– I hate love.

I knew these were all in direct contradiction to what the Bible says about love, that love is good:

> Love is patient, love is kind. It does not envy, it does not boast, it is not proud. It is not rude, it is not self-seeking, it is not easily angered, it keeps no record of wrongs. Love does not delight in evil but rejoices with the truth. It always protects, always trusts, always hopes, always perseveres. Love never fails.
>
> (1 Corinthians 13:4-8)

And this was the love that was pouring out of the team towards me. It *was* unconditional acceptance. It didn't change when I changed. It didn't take offence when I reacted angrily. It persevered and refused to give up.

Buried Roots

After every rude and angry outburst, of which there were many, I felt intensely guilty and ashamed. My bad attitudes and behavior became fresh fodder to reinforce the lie that I *was* bad at the core of my being. Again and again, I would spiral down into the cycle of bitter self-accusation and the desire to punish and harm myself.

But the God who says, "I desire mercy, not sacrifice" (Hosea 6:6) was working even through those times, to show me His heart that desires to bless, not to chastise. And I began to learn that He was calling me to look deeper than the sin issue that so devastated me. He had sent Jesus to pay the price for that.

His word to me was, "Come now, let us reason together" (Isaiah 1:18) as He called me to look not so much at *how* I responded to love, but *why* I responded the way I did. I needed to see the festering wound beneath the pus.

Gradually my heart softened and I began to dare to look with God at where this hatred of love came from, and why it was so deeply entrenched in me.

Although I was without the memory of my childhood, I knew I had been conceived before my parents were married, and my mother had told me repeatedly, even as an adult, that she wished she'd had me adopted. And there was no doubt that she favored my brother. Despite being expelled from school and detained both in borstal and prison, she always welcomed him back. She had told me that mothers always love their sons more than their daughters, and I believed her.

As I began to think tentatively about my mother's words and her attitude towards me, God began to work both directly and through the counseling team to help me embrace the truth that my mother had never loved me. It was a very hard truth to face.

Later on, I recovered excruciating memories of my father repeatedly sexually abusing me throughout my childhood. But it was not having any comfort from my mother that was, ultimately, the root of the deepest pain in my life. It was the very hardest thing for me to deal with on my journey to healing.

Sadly there are many, many people today who are victims of sexual abuse, which leaves devastating wounds. But I believe it is the cushioning around abuse that determines how deep those wounds go.

When there's no comfort, survival instinct kicks in. For me, this meant "chopping and blocking out" so much of my life, burying and denying what was too hard to embrace, and using my mind and strong will to keep it hidden. It was an extreme way of coping, even with sexual abuse, but it gave me a "safe place," a place where I didn't have to face the pain and devastation.

That was my comfort, and that was how these faulty beliefs had become so strong in my life, and why I found it so hard to receive the love I was desperate for. While I believed love was bad, I didn't have to face the truth that I was created to love and be loved (as we all are), and the truth of the pain of all that was withheld in my childhood, and the vacuum it had left within me. And while I believed I was bad, I could excuse my mother's attitude towards me, and avoid facing the pain of the injustice of being abused.

They were defenses, but they had been reinforced over a lifetime. It was as if they were set in concrete, and I couldn't simply let go of them. Everything in me told me that love wasn't right.

So, to begin with, the battle to receive love and to allow myself to have nice things, like the battle with food, was intense. But like water dripping on a stone that eventually wears it away, God continued to pour out His love and little by little my defenses began to lose their strength.

He wasn't working with the part of me that fought and argued and wanted to keep all the self-protection in place. That was the place of fear. He was working with my spirit which, when we are born again, is indwelt by God's Holy Spirit, and from where as children of the Living God we cry out "Abba,

Father" (Romans 8:15). He was reaching out to the place in me from which I was reaching out to Him.

It was a tender, fragile place, particularly in comparison to the strength of the fight in the rest of my being, but it was the place of truth, and God could work with that.

Note

A movement with overt phenomena that began in January 1994 at Toronto Airport Christian Fellowship and influenced many UK churches.

CHAPTER 3

A Stairway to Freedom

> You hem me in behind and before; you have laid your hand upon me ... Where can I go from your Spirit? Where can I flee from your presence? If I go up to the heavens, you are there; if I make my bed in the depths, behold, you are there. If I rise on the wings of the dawn, if I settle on the far side of sea, even there your hand will guide me, and your right hand will hold me fast.
>
> (Psalm 139:5, 7-10)

There is no doubt that God was with me. I knew His Holy Spirit was in me, leading and holding me. Yet at that time, although glimmers of light came into my darkness, as I grasped hold of something of the truth of the roots to my problems, or the truth of God's love, I couldn't seem to hold onto it, and would quickly slip back into negativity.

In my turmoil and confusion, I would sink under the weight of anxiety and despair, and God would, again, seem distant and unresponsive. I would struggle to believe that He was really there, or that there was a positive way forward that could lead to real freedom.

The Bible says that God "will repay you for the years the locusts have eaten" (Joel 2:25), but I couldn't understand how He could take away all the shame and fear I felt inside, and how He could ever make up for all that had been lost. I was despondent that I had landed up as a psychiatric patient, that the months were going into years of not being able to live a normal life, that my relationship with John and the children was so dysfunctional, and that my family were suffering.

For three years I hid indoors, either at home or at Ellel Grange or, to begin with, at the hospital as well. I had no life outside of those three places. A hospital minibus picked me up and took me door-to-door to and from the hospital. And when I went to Ellel Grange, although I was never afraid of being in the car on my own and driving the long distance, the car had to be filled to the brim with fuel, so that I wouldn't have to stop at a petrol station on the way. I felt contained and safe in the car. But I couldn't have traveled on a train or a coach, because the fear of people was so great.

Even though, in a sense, I had been rescued and was being rescued, hopelessness, fear of being out of control and an obsessive fear of people still gripped me. The fears seemed to flood up from a place deep inside, that I couldn't connect with and didn't understand. Yet the feelings were all-consuming, and I was frequently fighting a battle to resist the desperate urge to take my own life. It was a battle that would not have been won, had God's Holy Spirit not been with me and at work in me.

At the Bottom of a Well

It was as if I was still trapped at the bottom of a deep, dark well, and when I went back to Ellel Grange for extended visits, Fiona and Anna, and later others, were like a team of rescuers standing at the top of the well, shining flashlights down to me and calling down that there was a way out.

We would sit on the soft chairs in the room we always used for counseling. It was next door to my bedroom and had a window that looked out on a tall beech tree. I watched the tree change as the seasons came and went, and listened as time and again my counselors reassured me that I wasn't a nuisance, it wasn't hopeless and God had sent them to help me. They would remind me of the promises and faithfulness of God, reading out passages from the Bible such as:

> He has sent me to bind up the broken-hearted, to proclaim freedom for the captives, and release from darkness for the prisoners ... to comfort all who mourn ... to bestow on them a crown of beauty instead of ashes, the oil of gladness instead of mourning, and a garment of praise instead of a spirit of despair. They will be called oaks of righteousness, a planting of the Lord for the display of his splendor ...
>
> (Isaiah 61:1-3)

The Word of God reminded me that Jesus came to rescue, restore and redeem:

> I waited patiently for the Lord; he turned to me and heard my cry. He lifted me out of the slimy pit, out of the mud and mire; he set my feet on a rock and gave me a firm place to stand. He put a new song in my mouth – a hymn of praise to our God.
>
> (Psalm 40:1-3)

It reminded me that just as He had rescued the psalmist, David, His plan was to rescue me:

> "I have loved you with an everlasting love; I have drawn you with loving-kindness. I will build you up again and you will be rebuilt ..."
>
> (Jeremiah 31:3-4)

It reminded me that He'll always love me and always has, and it would be His love that would restore me:

> "You stretched out your right hand ... In your unfailing love you will lead the people you have redeemed. In your strength you will guide them ..."
>
> (Exodus 15:12-13)

It reminded me that He would lead me day by day as I looked
to Him:

> And my God will meet all your needs according to his glorious
> riches in Christ Jesus.
>
> (Philippians 4:19)

It reminded me that He would meet my every need even as
He rescued me:

> "Call to me and I will answer you and tell you great and unsearch-
> able things you do not know."
>
> (Jeremiah 33:3)

It reminded me that He would be listening whenever I called:

> "The thief comes only to steal and kill and destroy; I have come
> that they may have life, and have it to the full."
>
> (John 10:10)

It reminded me that there was a spiritual battle to fight, but
that Jesus had already won the victory for me, and that as I
came up out of the well there really would be freedom and
new life for me that would be exciting and fulfilling and exceed
any expectation I could have.

I was afraid of allowing myself to be vulnerable to anyone.
How could I let God or anyone else close to me, let them love
me? Even so, God was reaching down, feeding and nurturing
me, and pouring in His strength.

Yet the life-giving truth didn't seem to reach the place
of hopelessness. It was as if there was a gap, and the truth
couldn't flow into the place I most needed it.

I couldn't have understood it then, but it was all my own
defenses that were blocking the way. I had layers and layers of
coping mechanisms: the "chopping off and blocking out" of my
past, the obsessions with my body and my environment that
focused my attention at surface level and kept hidden realities
buried, the self-hatred, mistrust and fear. All of these things kept

the source of light and life that was flowing through my counselors to me from reaching the place I desperately needed it.

In time I would need to face up to and surrender them all,
but these things had helped me to keep a grip on life. I was
clinging to them and couldn't simply let them go.

A Way Out

But at the level that I was able to receive it, God's Word did
begin to take root. I was enabled by the Holy Spirit to embrace
it tentatively as truth: maybe the love and gentleness I saw in
these people's eyes, and all the time and patience they were
giving me really did mean they loved me. And if God had sent
them, then He must love me too.

Maybe I wasn't the failure I thought I was, and maybe I
wouldn't always have to live in this dark place of depression
with the constant dull ache of self-loathing. Maybe there were
reasons for the way I was, reasons that could be exposed and
healed. I began to grasp that even though I couldn't see it,
perhaps there was a way out for me.

It was as if my eyes began to make out steps cut into the
inner wall of the well, steps that spiraled up and round, and
looked as if they could lead all the way to the top to real
freedom. But I had to trust that they would continue all the
way up. Fear said they would lead me halfway up and then
run out, and I would be left on some dangerous precipice,
a place of abandonment by the people who were encouraging and supporting me. That felt like the worst thing
that could happen, and sometimes I desperately wanted
to take my own life rather than "climb the steps" and risk
that abandonment.

Life at Home

When I was at Ellel Grange with my counselors it wasn't so difficult to find hope. During each visit I grasped more of the truth of God's Word, that it was real and it was for me, and I began to learn to trust. As God enabled me by His Spirit, I was reaching up to Him and beginning to climb the spiraling steps.

But it was always a struggle when it was time to go back home. It was as if night fell and the rescuers with their flashlights left their posts at the top of the well and disappeared from my sight. The challenge was to hold on to the hope God had imparted through them, until my next visit to the Grange. After all I was never going home alone. The truth is that God was always with me, and He wanted me to learn to trust in His presence even, and perhaps especially, when it was hard.

After the three-hundred-mile journey home, I would walk through the door, virtually ignoring John, Tom and Beth, heading as if with tunnel vision straight to the sanctuary of my bedroom. I had slept alone in this room for years. I had always had a fear of physical intimacy even in our marriage, but after I broke down it became a complete anathema to me.

It was a desperately hard time for John. My dysfunction not only caused him pain, but put him under enormous strain as he sought to cope with the pressures of both a heavy workload and the demands of effectively being a single parent.

He went alone to attend school parents' evenings and to watch the children performing in concerts and plays, always reassuring them that "Mum will be better soon, and then she'll come too." He was selfless and steadfast in his belief that his job was to keep things as normal as possible for the children. From the bedroom I would hear him patiently telling them that I'd had a long journey home and it was best to let me rest.

I felt intensely guilty. I wanted to be able to give back to them something of the love they were extending to me by standing with me and not rejecting me through such difficult times. I would sit in my room and cry silently, and beat my legs violently to punish myself. But I still continued to push them away and isolate myself from them.

Before long I would cut myself off from what was going on in the rest of the house, and even from what was going on in my own life, as I became utterly preoccupied and obsessed with making sure every piece of furniture was perfectly lined up with the walls, every fold in the curtains even, and every ornament straight and in its place. I felt angry if anything was out of place, but underneath the anger was deep insecurity.

I would often sit up in bed late into the night journaling page after page in very neat handwriting. I filled up many, many notebooks and diaries. It somehow helped me to know I was alive and real. If I didn't write down the things I thought and felt, I somehow lost them and couldn't remember what I felt about anything.

Readjusting to being at home took at least a week. I was incommunicative and preoccupied, feeling as if I had been tipped out of the nest of Ellel Grange, and struggling to believe I wasn't a heap of rubbish, and the rescue team hadn't given up on me. In desperation to attach to the lifeline they had thrown, yet with an irrational fear of an angry response from them, I would reach a point of urgently begging John to phone Fiona or Anna, often late at night, to check they were still there for me. The fear of abandonment was so great that until I heard one of their voices reassuring me, I wanted to die.

John never doubted the integrity of the Ellel team and their commitment to us. He was and is my greatest encourager. He would patiently remind me of how privileged I was to be receiving this help, and gave endless reassurance that Fiona and the team hadn't forgotten me and would soon be in touch to arrange my next trip north.

Eventually I would settle down. These times at home were important. Without them I could easily have lost sight of the fact that my life was based at home with my family, and there would have been a danger that I could have become institutionalized, and wholly dependent on the team at Ellel Grange. As it was, I did ultimately develop an attachment disorder, about which I will share in a later chapter.

Being at home after the intensity of the counseling appointments, was also an opportunity to weigh and test the progress I was making. To begin with, I would feel as if nothing had changed, and there were many times when overwhelming guilt and sense of failure made me feel as if I had fallen right back down to the bottom of the well. In reality I sometimes took two steps forward and one back, but it was never two steps forward and two back. God was sowing in His love and revealing the truth of my life, and no matter how painful that became, somewhere deep down it brought a sense of relief and hope. He was always graciously leading me on, and in His mercy covering John and the children.

Having readjusted and begun to feel safe at home, about a week before I was due to go back to Ellel Grange, fear and anxiety would grip me again, and making the decision about whether or not to go dominated my thought life and journal entries. It was always a battle but, by God's grace, I never missed an appointment.

The Work of Rebuilding and Dismantling

With John by my side at home, and the team at Ellel Grange, together with the strength that the truth of God's Word was imparting, it was as if God had put scaffolding all around, to support and protect me, so that He could begin His work of dismantling. Like taking down flawed walls that endanger the safety of a building, He began to dismantle the lies I had always believed. My eyes were opened to the truth that:

- my parents' behavior towards me wasn't normal, and my relationship with them wasn't as God intended;

- there was more to my loss of memory of the first eighteen years of my life than a simple character weakness;

- my self-loathing, fears, problems with food and obsessive compulsive behavior were symptomatic of a deeper problem.

I had accepted Fiona and the team's offer to receive ongoing help because, despite the fear, I hadn't wanted to run away from reality anymore. Although for a long time it had enabled me to function in life and keep up the appearance of normality, in the end I had crashed. I had become exhausted by it, and the truth was that things weren't normal. I knew that whatever was in my past, it had a hold over me, and I was finally ready to face it so that I could get free.

This meant letting go of the tapes I played over and over again in my head, tapes that said things like: "I'm OK really. I'm just attention-seeking. I need to get my act together." It meant agreeing to the team praying for God to shine the light of truth on my life, and being willing to embrace whatever He revealed.

I had two major fears: the first was a very real fear of deception and, the second, a fear of being out of control, but God had been painstakingly laying a foundation of trust in me, both in Him and in the counseling team. Fearfully I put my hand in His and made a conscious choice to believe that He would be in control.

CHAPTER 4

Broken Childhood

I was climbing another step up the inner wall of the well, and as the team prayed, it was as if I came to a place where there was a closed door set back in the wall, a door I hadn't been able to see until I reached this place. It had been locked for many years and this was the time for it to be opened. Sitting on the sofa with my eyes closed, I battled with whether to keep going, or to agree with the conflicting thoughts in my head that said this wasn't real. The team continued to pray and I set my will to keep going.

Behind Locked Doors

As an adult sitting in the room that day, there came a moment when I wasn't aware of what was going on around me anymore. My eyes were closed and, for me, it was almost as if I fell asleep. But what the team who were praying (with their eyes open) saw, at that same moment, was a sudden switch in me. I went from being an adult sitting up straight with my eyes closed to an extremely traumatized child, curled up in a tight ball in the corner of the sofa. This child was a part of my personhood which the "adult me" had no connection with. It was as if the door in the wall had opened onto a cold, dark, windowless cell, where a lost and terrified child was imprisoned.

Fiona and Anna spoke gently and compassionately, "It's all right. You're safe. Jesus has sent us to help you." But, as a three-year-old child, I was panic-stricken and at first unable to receive their reassurance. I couldn't move and was too frightened to open my eyes. I was shaking and holding my hands up, trying desperately to protect myself. This little child was oblivious of the inconsistency of being in a big adult body. She was oblivious of virtually everything in her physical surroundings. It felt as if I was still in the bedroom of the flat where my Dad was molesting me, and I was trying so hard to run away in my head to "the nothing place," my escape place, where I didn't feel or see or hear anything.

This was the broken part of me that was locked in Dissociative Identity Disorder and carried the experience, the memory and the truth of the first three years of my life. The team had seen a clear switch, not just in the manifestation of trauma, but in my responses and demeanor, to that of a small child. They could see without doubt this was still me, and I was very real, but I was different and I didn't know them. Except that we shared the same 37-year-old body, as a child I was completely separate from the adult the team had known thus far. Thirty-four years after I had broken away from myself at three years old, I was still locked in the prison of the moment of my father's cruel abuse that was so severe it had caused the breaking. The clock had stopped for me in this part.

With the utmost sensitivity, Fiona and Anna spoke God's words of compassion, safety and comfort. The gentleness and tenderness of their voices, and the care I saw in their eyes when I dared to look, gave me the confidence to begin to let out the screams and sobs I had needed to release for so many years.

Although as a fragmented part I hadn't been conscious of the passing of the years, I had nevertheless been buried in darkness for a very long time, during which I had never seen the light of day, nor related with anyone else. It wasn't just the pain of my parents' abuse that was locked in this part of me, but the injustice of all that I had missed out on as a little child. There had been no normality, no freedom to run and play and be with other children. There was a starvation for love and relationship, and at the same time huge fear and inability to trust.

This little child part of me, who became known as Sarah 3,[1] needed a lot of help, but after a short time I closed my eyes and slipped back down to the subconscious level. The team, witnessing again the switch, instantly saw before them a shaken and confused "adult Sarah."

For Sarah 3, it had been a big shock to suddenly find herself in a new world, and it had taken a lot of courage to dare to let go of the screams and sobs that came from the old world, but it had also been a huge relief. God had done His work for that time. Through Fiona and Anna's kindness and gentleness He had put a tiny seed of hope into this broken child part, just as He had done in the "adult me" through my first visit to Ellel Grange.

As the "adult me," I opened my eyes as if waking from unconsciousness. I sat up straight and looked at my counselors in bewilderment, not knowing what had taken place while I had been "asleep."

At appropriate times and with the agreement of the "adult me," the team would ask God to bring "three-year-old Sarah" to the surface again, so that they could continue to minister His healing. And when my initial fears eventually subsided, as Sarah 3, I clung to Fiona and the comfort she offered. "I want my mummy to hug me," I cried to her over and over again, with the voice of a three-year-old child. And over and over again she would tell me that Jesus had wanted my Mummy to hug me, too, and He was cross that she hadn't.

It wasn't that my mother didn't know I was being abused or that she didn't know how to bring comfort. The truth I was eventually able to share, with the heartfelt pain and anger of a child, was that my mother, who had never wanted or loved me, blamed and punished me for my father's abuse.

As a broken part I couldn't sustain more than an hour or so in today's world. It would become a strain, and I would get tired and want to switch back to allowing the "adult me" back in the driving seat. The team worked hard during the times they had, to bring as much love and safety as they could to Sarah 3.

It Can't Be True!

Whenever the "adult me" came back, the only idea I had of what had transpired during the time I had lost, derived from the way my body felt or from the evidence around me. Sometimes my eyes were wet from crying, or my throat sore from shouting. Sometimes there was an empty glass on the table in front of me, and I knew I must have had a drink. I hated suddenly finding myself sitting cross-legged on the floor and not knowing how I got there, or not knowing what I had been saying or why I had been crying or shouting, and would often question whether I really was a complete "nutcase."

There was such a confusion of emotion. I felt disorientated, and the realization that I had not been in control made me angry. But underneath the anger was fear: fear of what I might have said, and fear of having made a fool of myself. Yet in amongst all this there was a very real sense of relief that came from inside, because something in me (Sarah 3) was being released and healed.

The team would gently share with me all that had happened. To begin with, despite their sensitivity, I was shocked. For so many years I had lived out of an idealized view of my childhood, and it felt like some shameful, dirty secret being uncovered. I didn't want any of what they were telling me to be true.

It took time to come to terms with reality. After one of the early times Fiona and Anna spent with my three-year-old self, as the "adult me" I wrote in my journal:

> *Fiona ministered to fragmented 3-year-old. I found it too painful – too frightening. I felt suicidal. I wanted to escape. I hate myself. I feel as though there may be other fragmented parts at other ages. It all seems too hard, too much to think about. I just want to shut those parts off. I didn't feel safe so I gave Anna my drugs.*

Flashbacks and Fainting

As the "adult me" I began to have graphic and horrifying flashbacks of abuse. They came as a huge shock to my system, and for several weeks I became physically very unwell. Migraine attacks became frequent and lasted for several days at a time. I found it difficult to sleep, was unable to eat much and became very weak, fainting regularly.

It was an enormous struggle to believe that these were true pictures of what had happened to me as a child. And it was a struggle to allow Fiona and the team close. I wanted to push everyone away and shut myself in the bedroom, but most of the time it wasn't safe for me to do this, because I was extremely suicidal.

I argued stubbornly with my counselors that I must be suffering from some form of "false memory syndrome." I wanted to go back to believing that I simply had a bad memory – nothing else. I wanted to slam shut that door that had been opened and begged the team many times to pray for God to reveal to them any deception that was somehow operating in me. They went away and prayed but there was no revelation of deception.

Instead, God gave Fiona a picture of a rose that had been smashed, with the petals strewn all over the ground. He said He was going to pick up each petal and gather them together and lovingly restore the rose to wholeness. It was a beautiful picture that touched me deeply. And there were many times to come when I would turn my thoughts back to that image to give me the encouragement I needed, to combat the doubt and unbelief that bombarded my mind, and to keep pressing on.

Seven Shattered Parts

During the time I was experiencing the flashbacks, the team continued to pray with me and, one by one, six more "prison doors" were revealed, behind which were six more "parts": a baby, two child parts aged nine and twelve, and three teenage parts aged sixteen, seventeen and eighteen. Together with Sarah 3, these were the shattered parts that were locked in Dissociative Identity Disorder, the parts that held all the memories that were lost to the "adult me."

Through my parents' sustained cruelty and neglect, each part had been robbed of innocence, self-respect, living the life of a child, running free and making friends. And as each door was opened, my counselors saw the switch between the "adult me" and each traumatized, broken part, in which they witnessed the same terror, the same inability to trust and the same deep sense of utter worthlessness and despair.

At three years of age, in that extreme moment of sexual abuse, I had broken away from the three-year-old part of myself that held all the memory, pain and anguish of my parents' depravity and cruelty. I had left behind the imprisoned, traumatized Sarah 3, who was now being rescued. The truth of my past was being brought into the light.

After the breaking, I had continued on in the day-to-day life of my childhood, still subject to my father's repeated violent and incestuous acts, and my mother's hatred. There came a point at nine years of age when I broke again, and in my nine-year-old part (Sarah 9) were all the memories, pain and anguish of the years between three and nine. And so it went on until I was eighteen and the abuse finally stopped.

Each part held the memories of all that had happened in my life from the time of the previous breaking up to the age I then was. Each part of me was separate, and until the time when God later began to draw us closer together, there was no flowing of information between one part and another. This meant that if God didn't fulfill His promise and put the "rose petals" back together, as the "adult me" living everyday life, I would never be able to access the memory of my life before the age of eighteen.

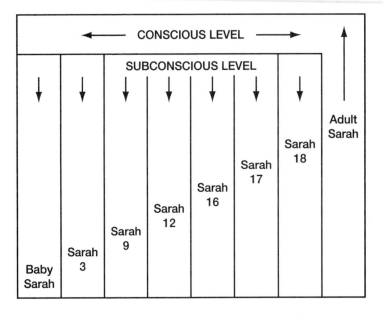

Figure 2. Diagram illustrating the "adult me" at the conscious level, whilst all my other broken parts were hidden/compartmentalized.

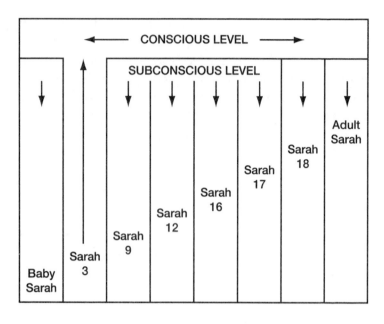

Figure 3. Now after a switch, "Sarah 3" has come up to the conscious level, whilst "adult me" has gone down and, like all my other broken parts, is hidden in the subconscious.

Danger of Death

At eighteen I had suffered the most extreme abuse, and in this part (Sarah 18) I felt so dirty and believed against all rationale that the abuse was my fault. I hated myself with a vengeance and was intent on punishing and harming myself. I was utterly heartbroken by all I had lost, and intensely suicidal. In the "adult me" I had learned how important it was that I fixed my will to be obedient to the ways of God. His Word told me to "choose life ..." (Deuteronomy 30:19), yet there was this part of me, Sarah 18, who had never known God and His love, and who didn't just feel like dying, but had a will and seriously wanted to commit suicide.

Although brokenness kept a separation between us, as the "adult me" living life I often struggled to cope with the pressure of Sarah 18's feelings that came through from the inside. Instead of being understanding and compassionate towards her, I was angry. It felt as if it was her fault that I had such a big struggle with the compulsive urge to self-destruct. And there were dangerous times when I genuinely, desperately wanted to give in to the desire, and blame her. I knew this would be wrong because, whether I liked it or not, wanted it or not, I was responsible for my broken parts. In truth they were part of me.

There were times when my frustration reached explosion point. I didn't want to be broken in parts. I didn't want to have been sexually abused, to feel so ashamed and dirty and repulsed. I didn't want to be desperate for a mother, to feel so pathetic. And I was so intensely afraid that somehow I was making it all up, and if I was, I was terrified of what a bad, bad person that would make me.

With this tormenting confusion of inner conflict, there was one occasion when I completely abdicated my adult responsibility and agreed with Sarah 18 that suicide was the only answer. I left her with no place of safety, no umbrella of hope under which to hide.

Instead of remaining on the surface, as the "adult me," and being honest with my counselors about the seriousness of the desperate place Sarah 18 was in, so that they could bring God's comfort to her and she could be strengthened, I allowed her, in her hopeless suicidal state, to "come up" when no one else was there. Sarah 18, at that point, was completely vulnerable to her own feelings and took a severe overdose of painkillers, which put the whole person in serious danger of death.

An intensely worrying time followed for everyone. I believe it was only God's mercy that caused repeated bouts of vomiting throughout the night, so that the potentially lethal overdose was cleansed from my system.

Recovery and Accountability

When I had recovered enough physically, the team, firmly yet sensitively, called the "adult me" to account: where in my heart had I chosen to go against the will of God, in such a way that I had left Sarah 18 so vulnerable? I was angry and argued with the team. I didn't want to take the blame: "It wasn't '*me*' who took the overdose! It was '*her*'!" It felt intensely unfair, and I wanted to run away from Ellel Grange and escape back to my home …

But what would I have done then? There was only one hope, and it was in the God whose heart was to lift me into life, and who desired and planned the very best for me. He was initiating His rescue plan through these people, not because I deserved it, but because of His great love for me. With a repentant heart, I climbed down from my high horse, recognizing the wrong choice I had made. I knew I had hurt God by choosing my own way over His, and I humbly came before Him and said sorry.

I learned a hard lesson: however tough this walk was, it was never about God making strict rules that were too hard to keep, and it was never right to sink down into self-pity and "how hard this is for me." God was rescuing me and, in His mercy, had put people around me to support me, and He was there with His grace, calling me to draw on that grace that would lead me into the freedom I longed for.

Note

1.   The 3 refers to the age I was when this dissociation took place.

——————⟨⟩◆⟨⟩——————

CHAPTER 5

Embracing Parts I Didn't Want

There were times when the mist cleared and, as the "adult me," I could see the reality of my brokenness, and the reasons for it. I knew what I had seen in the flashbacks, and I had a sense of the truth of my past, although I was still without the clarity of memory.

I was relieved that finally there were logical reasons for all the things that otherwise didn't make any sense: my absence of eighteen years of memories all my life, the battles with suicidal thoughts and tendencies, landing up in a psychiatric hospital being prescribed such heavy dosages of drugs and, ultimately, needing such intense counseling. God's revelation of my broken parts, who carried all the memories, made sense of life for me.

A Lifestyle of "Chopping and Blocking"

However, my lifetime's survival mechanisms had become so much a part of me they didn't just lay down and die. I was a person who had gone to the extreme of protecting myself by "chopping off and blocking out" not just memories but parts of my very self. I ran away from things that would otherwise have devastated me.

It was how I had coped from the earliest age. When my father was violent and abused me, and my mother hated and blamed me, I was left with nowhere to turn, so I ran away to "the nothing place" in my head. And as I grew up, separating from the truth of my own brokenness was how I got by. Believing I was all right, and absorbing myself in keeping my environment obsessively tidy to reinforce that belief, protected me from the pain I couldn't face. This pattern of coping was firmly entrenched, and it didn't just fall away.

Although I was learning to trust, and wanted to trust God, the reality was that I still trusted my own mechanisms more than anything or anyone else. When fear rose up, it outweighed faith and I was frantic to gain back the control I had handed over to God. I would, unwittingly, distance myself from the cruel, unjust reality, and argue with my counselors that these child parts weren't real, convincing myself at the same time that there was nothing wrong with me. When I put my will to this, my mind had enormous strength that worked against the truth God was exposing.

At such times the team would have the difficult job of prodding the pain and reality, lovingly confronting me with questions that would burst my bubble of unreality and bring me back to the truth: Why are you so obsessed with keeping everything in immaculate order? Why are you so desperate for a mother? Why can't you sleep with your husband?

Self-abandonment Caused Further Suffering

I began to understand that it wasn't just my parents who had abused and abandoned me. The truth was that I had abandoned me. In my adult place, I had used my mind to shut away parts of my own self (child and teenage), locked them up and thrown away the key. I had learnt to live without them. As the help I was receiving progressed, I was continuing to hurt and punish them (myself) every day that went by, when I slipped back into denying their existence, begrudged "switching over" to allow them time and refused to embrace them as me.

It wasn't easy to face up to this, because the reality was that, even then, I still didn't want to embrace and own parts that carried horrors of a past I didn't want to be mine.

I would have found it easier if the team had given the parts different names, like "Passive Sarah" and "Angry Sarah": names that described their attitudes. I would have found it easier if my counselors hadn't called them parts of me at all, but related with them individually as separate alternative personalities.

I could have left God and the counseling team to relate with each one in the compartmentalized space behind those locked doors, while I kept my distance and abdicated any responsibility for them. I could have lived my life separately from them and blamed "Angry Sarah" for her angry outbursts and "Passive Sarah" for her passivity. And I could have felt justified in hating and rejecting them, while, as the adult, I worked at "being good."

However, God's Word convicted me that my way was not His way:

> "...We have made a lie our refuge and falsehood our hiding-place."
>
> (Isaiah 28:15)

> I appeal to you, brothers, in the name of our Lord Jesus Christ, that all of you agree with one another so that there may be no divisions among you and that you may be perfectly united in mind and thought.
>
> (1 Corinthians 1:10)

And the picture God had given wasn't one that promised to help me to learn to live as several people, all occupying one body. It was a picture of the scattered and damaged petals of *one* whole rose, being restored back to one *whole* rose as He originally intended.

Self-acceptance – Key to Healing

The vast majority of the time the Ellel team spent with me was not with my broken parts but with the "adult me," who needed to relinquish denial and unreality, and embrace the whole truth of my past, that was mined with pain.

It was important to get to the place where I could take rightful responsibility and trust God afresh for the part I had played (however small that had been) in choosing to separate from the child parts that carried the traumas. Some people would argue that, in the face of such extreme abuse, the breaking was an involuntary action, so there was nothing to say sorry for.

I stood my ground with this argument myself for a long time, but ultimately came to a place of recognizing that, as human beings, we make choices in everything we do, and that to some very small degree I had made a choice, perhaps even a subconscious choice, but nevertheless a choice, to escape from pain by separating from myself.

I realized that I needed a real change of heart. Instead of wanting to be separate from my fragmented parts and have nothing to do with them, I needed to be open to seeing them as parts of me. Instead of hating them and rejecting them, I needed to see them with compassion, to begin to like them, to truly desire to say sorry to them for separating from them and to really want them.

Grudgingly I had allowed the team to build relationships with them, but there came a point where God was asking the *"adult me"* to take on that responsibility for myself – to take rightful responsibility for my broken parts. I needed a change of heart towards them, to care about how they felt, their needs, their desires, and to embrace them. Freedom from fears and obsessions, self-hatred and suicidal tendencies could only come if I, ultimately, allowed those locked doors to remain fully open, and embraced each part wholly as me. This had to be a work of God's grace in me. I knew I couldn't do it without the help of His Holy Spirit.

I learned to make a deliberate choice every day to pray for *Holy Spirit* to be in control of which part of me was on the surface, "living, being and relating" at any given time. This went against my natural desires, because by this time I realized that, by closing my eyes and slipping into the subconscious, I was capable of "switching" between being in the "here and now" as the "adult me" and forcing one of my broken parts to take over, and I could easily have chosen this as a means of escape.

There were many times when, as the "adult me," I wanted to run away from situations that touched my pain: like seeing a child being held tenderly in his or her mother's arms (something I had been denied). I wanted to "switch" and force a child part to deal with the pain instead of having to face it myself as the "adult me," but I had learned from the incident when Sarah 18 overdosed that it would have been dangerous to have given in to those temptations and to have abdicated my responsibility. Just as Sarah 18 had done before, a younger part might have chosen to take pills, self-harm or run away, if I had forced one of them to face something God wasn't asking her to face.

It wasn't easy to continue to allow God to be in control, and to stay and face the underlying pain, the truth of the injustice of my past that had had such a devastating outworking in my life. But God is a Redeemer and, hard as it was, through those times He was reaching out to me with His love and compassion, His grace and mercy, and teaching me the reality of His all-sufficiency in the place of pain and suffering. I share more about this later.

Healing the Broken Parts

My counselors spent periods of time with each broken part, gently encouraging each one to talk about her feelings and to receive the love God wanted to pour in.

I realized that sharing, crying, laughing, playing and eating together are the natural ways God intends children to receive love through normal family life. And His heart was to put back into me, through His family, what was needed to rebuild my self-respect, personal worth and value, trust and relationship skills, so that one day each part would be ready to grow up and be joined together as one, and enter into all the fullness of life.

Each part had the same battle with hating love because it had such bad connotations and felt so untrustworthy. Yet there was always a longing for love because, in the end, it truly is an undeniable God-given need. The Spirit of adoption (Romans 8:15-16) in the "adult me" and in each child part, too, was reaching out to God. It was the work of His Holy Spirit in me that, ultimately, enabled all my broken parts to bond with Fiona and Anna and others in the team. They in turn introduced each one to Jesus.

To begin with, in each part I made angry protestations: "Where was Jesus when my dad was making me take my clothes off? Where was He when he made me touch him? Why didn't Jesus stop him? Why didn't He help me?" Sarah 18, who struggled so hard to come to terms with the degradation and heart-wrenching losses, put up the biggest fight.

But the team remained steadfast in my rage. They responded with gentleness, explaining to each part individually that Jesus was there with me all the time, but He couldn't overrule my parents' choices.

They shared, too, how He had been stripped naked, whipped and nailed to a cross, and knew what it was like to be mocked, bleeding, hurting and alone. In each part this touched me deeply. It was such a relief to find there was someone who completely understood the anguish and the inhumanity of my early life. Each part grasped the reality that Jesus loves us so much that He chose to identify Himself with suffering children and suffering people, so that He could take our pain and we could be healed and set free (Isaiah 53:3-5).

In each part I knew He was the one I needed. I knew it especially in Sarah 18. No one else and nothing else was sufficient for the pain in this part. Abuse didn't just feel as if it was something that had happened to me. It felt as if it *was* me: it had had such a devastating effect and had been so integral in forming the person I had become. It was very hard to let go of the losses and the pain, but I cried out to Jesus and it was God's Holy Spirit who enabled me to lay it at the cross, and to finally put my trust in Him to meet my needs from thereon in.

Abuse had deposited its filth on me to such an extent that I had believed, in every part, that I was dirty to the core of my being. I had been bitter and angry and jealous of others, but all the darkness was washed away, and light and love came into those prison cells. For the first time each part knew she was loved, each part had peace in place of torment and real hope to cling to. It was a miracle that only God, through the team He had appointed, could have wrought.

People sometimes ask, "What would have happened if your child parts had rejected Jesus?" The answer is, I wouldn't have survived. But it is also true that, because as an adult I had received Jesus as my Savior and my broken parts were all part of me, albeit separate parts, in reality it would have been impossible for each part not to have had the same heart, and not to have accepted Him. I am so grateful, for I did not choose Him, but He chose me (John 15:16).

Working Together

As each broken part received healing into the traumas and was no longer in a place of abject pain, they were also being released from the lonely isolation they had always known. They began to become more aware of one another and, because of this, each part, including "adult Sarah," began to call ourselves "we" instead of "I."

Although all seven parts shared one physical body, and only one part could relate with other people who were with them at any one time, it didn't mean that the other parts ceased to exist when they were hidden. During the times the team spent with each part, they encouraged them to sense how the other "underneath" parts were feeling, to develop a love and care for one another, and to pray for one another. In this way, there developed a unity through learning to "work together" as a team.

When one part was struggling with overwhelming pain, God would often bring another one to the surface to tell the counseling team, so that she could help the suffering part cry out her pain to Jesus and receive His comfort. Ultimately, each part learned to work in harmony with the others, and to stand against the powers of darkness that hated the work of love and healing God was doing. Miraculously each one came to a place of completely forgiving my parents.

Even though as "adult Sarah" I continued to battle with owning my fragmented parts as part of me, in each broken part I had compassion for "adult Sarah." Each part easily forgave "adult Sarah" for breaking away, and felt for me in my struggles, because they knew I had had to carry on and cope in life while they were hidden. They were always for me, praying from the inside.

Time for Each Part

There was more for each part than simply being rescued from the dark prisons they had been in. God's heart was to wholly release each one, initially individually, into the rich and full life Jesus has won for every one of us on the cross (John 10:10). He wanted me to find myself, to know who I am, to truly answer my heart cry of "Who am I?" So, each part was given time to discover her own uniqueness, her likes and dislikes, and to do what she wanted to do.

At first this was in the counseling setting, but as the "adult me" became more confident in listening to God's Spirit and knowing when it was safe and appropriate, during times on my own at home I would "switch" and allow my broken parts time to "just be."

I had never played before, and God knew I could never grow up to be a well-rounded, whole adult if I hadn't learned to play as a three-year-old, or to relate as a twelve-year-old, or express my feelings as a teenager.

In my adult body, yet in every other way as a three-year-old, I played with dolls and paints. Sarah 3 saw herself running and jumping and skipping along beside Jesus on what she called "the sunshine road." As a three-year-old, I knew Jesus was pleased that I was happy, and I knew I could talk to Him when I was sad. I knew it was all right to be sad about my parents, but I knew too that I could trust Him, and that He would never, ever leave me. There could be no greater contrast in this picture of love and being loved against the cold, isolated place of darkness He had rescued me from.

Sarah 9 loved seashells and made collages, sticking shells and colored beads on to paper and painting them. As Sarah 12, I learned to play the piano – something I had never done before. Sarah 16 experimented with make-up, Sarah 17 loved flowers and nature, whilst Sarah 18 did lots of creative writing.

Figure 4.
Drawing, Sarah Age 3.

Figure 5.
Letter to Fiona, Sarah Age 9.

At various times, each part did some writing and, to begin with, as "adult Sarah" I was stunned to see that the handwriting of each part was appropriate to her age. Sarah 3 could write her name, but sometimes wrote some of the letters back to front. Sarah 9's writing was much more developed, and Sarah 12's even more so but still contained some spelling mistakes, and my teenage parts' writing became much smaller and neater with a much greater vocabulary.

My fragmented parts all had very precious and important times that helped them to grow in their self-worth. Sometimes people think it must have been fun to "pop up" as a young child and then an older child, an adolescent and back to an adult again. It is true that each part did experience times of enjoyment, fun and laughter, but living as a broken person is never fun.

I used to think I couldn't do anything any good but Jesus has given me lots of friends and He has helped me to do music and writing and cross stitch. He has shown me that I can be happy and He helps me if I am sad and he shows me that I can help other people as well when I pray for them and make things for them and I think maybe when I talk to them.

Sarah Age 12

"I'm giving you a family,"
This new friend says to me,
"We love you and we care for you,
We'll never go away."

"Can this be true?" confused, I ask,
Dare I trust in Him?
A future and a hope at last?
I long to know it's really true and they won't abandon me.

Sarah Age 16

and afraid - so afraid that you wish you could die rather than face living another moment. Those were bad times but I don't want to think about them. I want to write about what Jesus is doing for me - well, for all of us - there are 7 of us - we are aged 3, 9, 12, 16, 17, 18 and grown up.

Sarah Age 17

We were hopeless: without hope. We wanted to die. Everything good was hidden from us. But we weren't hidden from Jesus. We didn't know that because we didn't know him. But He knew me,

Sarah Age 18

Figure 6. The handwriting of Sarah's "fragmented parts".

It was always a struggle to let go of my own control, to switch and allow my broken parts time. And, in embracing brokenness, I could never get away from the reasons for it. I wished with all my heart that I had been an uninhibited, care-free child, who enjoyed wearing her hair in bunches, sitting cross-legged on the floor and playing with a pot of bubbles – at the time God intended me to be. There was always a sadness underlying the joy of doing these things, because it was out of the natural order of time.

And although I did my best to be sensitive to John, it wasn't easy for him to cope with the times when I was very obviously a child. It wasn't easy either for him to come to terms with the collection of teddy bears, dolls and childlike paintings that all became so important to me, and were clear reminders around the home that his wife wasn't wholly adult.

The truth is that this was never God's best plan for my life, although I am so thankful that, in His mercy, it was His redemptive plan, through which He worked miracles in these shattered parts of my personality. Ultimately, each one was able to relate with the counseling team as a normal, healthy child of the age we each were.

Growth and Joining Together

The goal, of course, was always growing together to be one whole person as God originally intended. As "adult Sarah" I was very fearful of this. I only knew how to live by compart-mentalizing everything: when I was alone at home I would switch and allow "Sarah 3" to play with her toys. After a while she would "go down" and "adult Sarah" would come back. I would tidy away the toys and cook the dinner. Somehow that worked for me. We were all separate and we all did sepa-rate things.

As "adult Sarah" I wasn't spontaneous, and never had been. Everything was so controlled, and I couldn't imagine what being all joined together as one would be like. I was afraid I wouldn't know how to be myself and how to behave. I was afraid I would somehow be out of control.

In each part, there were fears about growth. Sarah 18 wrote this:

One day Jesus will ask me to grow up and this is the most fearful thing of all for me. He has rescued me and healed me from the most terrible things, delivered me and set me free, but I have to recognize that He never intended me to be broken and locked out of time. I am 18 years old in a body that is naturally growing older. He is a God of order, not of chaos and confusion, and He created me, like everyone else, to be one person – whole, united and at peace with myself and Him.

But I am to grow from 18 to 38 through one quick prayer. It's true that I was lost. But now I'm found, I'm me. I'm learning to be a person in my own right. I've found myself and I felt angry that I'm going to have to be joined to the others. I want to be me now. I don't want to be someone else. Jesus has given me friends. I'm afraid of losing them. Will people still want to spend time with me when I'm 20 years older? I'm so afraid I'll be different and I won't be me.

Jesus showed me the others and I felt angry. I wanted to push them away with all my strength, and shout at them, "No! Get away! Don't touch me! Don't come near! Don't try to be part of me. Let me have this life!" They just looked at me, each alone and expressionless.

I looked at the younger ones. I've never had a past and that's OK. I looked at adult Sarah and I wanted to scream, "No, no, no! Please, no!" I don't want to be her. I'll be lost again. She's married. She has children. No, I don't want that. I shook in fear and panic and thought of the children I should have had, and the abuse I had suffered. No, I don't want her children or the touch of her husband.

A voice, so quietly and so gently, whispered to me, "Those people who each stand as islands, expressionless and lonely, are you." I didn't want to hear it. I tried to close my ears to it, and I saw what looked like huge square pieces of metal about to come down between me and each of those isolated figures. I cried out to Jesus, "Hold me! Please, hold me!" I reached out my hand and asked Him to take it. "Please, Lord Jesus, take my hand. Hold my hand." He stood close by and looked into my eyes and He looked lovingly at the others, who each looked so alone, and He said, "Hold their hands. Then, you'll be holding Mine.' I was horrified. "No! I want You, Jesus, not them." He looked at me again, and said, "If you love them, you are loving Me. If you hold their hands, you are holding Mine."

Everything in me was fighting against His words. I felt as if I would be lost again, I wouldn't be me anymore. I'd be grown up. There'd be no choice anymore. I was heartbroken.

Trembling in fear, I called out to Him to help me to reach out to clasp the hands of those lonely figures.

It was so scary, but He helped me. He was right there with me, and we stood in a circle holding hands, looking at one another, all silently asking, "Do you accept me? Do I belong?" None of us rejected any other.

Jesus showed me straight away that this was all there was to it. He had asked me to do something very hard and I had been so fearful of the consequences, but He didn't have any hidden agendas. He was entirely trustworthy. I reached out my hand in obedience and that was love. It was an act of love, and then I felt an overwhelming feeling of love for Jesus, and I wanted more than ever to do whatever He asked me to do. I asked Him to fill my heart with love for the others, to give me a desire to not just tentatively reach out my hand to them in obedience, but to open my arms wide to welcome them and embrace them and love them. I want my heart to be a reflection of His.

This was the beginning of each part accepting and embracing all the other parts, and growing together to be the whole person God intended me to be.

There was still more work to do in "adult Sarah" before this full joining could take place. But the time was to come when, in embracing my fragmented parts, I would be embracing myself and fully accepting my past as part of who I am. In so doing the horrors of abuse and neglect would no longer have any power over me. (I share how this happened in my final chapter.)

CHAPTER 6

The Truth of My Early Years

Through the flashbacks and through all that the counseling team shared with the "adult me" of their times with my child parts, who together carried the complete memory of my upbringing, for the first time I began to gain a true picture of my early life. And later on, with the joining together of all my fragmented parts, I gained the uninterrupted full memory of all my childhood and teenage years.

School-days

At school I had been a loner and what teachers called "reticent." I had tried to be invisible, staring down at my desk or the floor, my cheeks burning, willing the teachers not to pick on me for an answer when they asked the class a question. It wasn't that I didn't know the answer – I was just afraid to speak.

I wasn't an obviously distressed child whose work suffered, or a rebellious one like my younger brother Mark who was often in trouble at school and later with the police. He hit out at others with his pain and frustration, but I hid mine inside, and set my strong will to be good and work hard. My school reports contained words like "hardworking" and "painstaking," alongside the more insightful comments of "lacking in confidence" and "withdrawn."

At playtimes I watched from a distance the other children running and playing with skipping ropes and tennis balls in the playground, and secretly wanted to join in. But I kept my head bowed and watched from under my fringe, afraid of even making eye contact, because I couldn't let anyone close. There would be too many questions, and too many answers I couldn't give.

At the end of the school-day children ran to their mothers, who were waiting for them in the playground, and greeted them with smiles and hugs and excited chatter. My mother met me and my brother in the playground too, but there wasn't a smile or a word exchanged between us. We weren't allowed to speak in public. It was rude. So we walked home in silence.

I knew we weren't like other children and our home and family were different, but I pretended it wasn't. That's what my mother did, too. Although we had very little money, she dressed us well and we were always clean and tidy. We were trained to be well behaved and polite, and not to speak unless spoken to. And we were punished at home with a beating from my father if we did.

My mother kept people at a distance. When neighbors spoke to her she gave them a curt reply. Later she would tell us they were nosey and interfering and we were not to talk to them. And both my brother and I knew without asking that we were never allowed to have any friends home from school or to visit anyone else's home.

I lived in a make-believe world in my head where I pretended everything was OK and I was OK, and I pretended I didn't live in fear of anyone finding out the truth.

A Violent Home

The truth was that our home was extremely dysfunctional. My father was angry and aggressive, and there were often raging arguments and violent struggles between my parents.

My brother and I knew when a fight was brewing. I would run and sit curled up at the top of the stairs. Mark would climb into bed and hide under the blankets. He often fell asleep in the middle of a fight, but I was always gripped by fear for my mother's safety and listened intently to the bitter exchanges.

During one incident, my father threatened my mother that he was going to "break every bone in her body" because he was suspicious that she was having an affair, although she wasn't. Sometimes he came thundering up the stairs and deflected his anger onto me, giving me a beating, just for listening. At other times he would storm out, slamming the door loudly behind him, and leave us ... but he always came back.

There were other times when his anger was solely directed at either my brother or me. His dark eyes would bulge, and looked as if they were going to burst out of their sockets. He was a heavy, thick-set, strong man with powerful arms and big, thick-fingered hands. He would grab one of us and beat us, and we would keep repeating over and over again, "I'm sorry, I'm sorry." We didn't know what we had done to make him angry, or what we were saying sorry for, except that we wanted him to stop.

Sexual Abuse

But, for me, worse than the beatings was the sexual abuse, which began when I was three years old. My father was self-employed and worked at repairing motorbikes in his lean-to workshop adjacent to our house. Whenever my mother left me alone, he came indoors, smelling of sweat and engine oil, and abused me to satisfy his own depraved sexual pleasure. He was such a frightening man I did whatever he asked me to do, even repeating after him that I liked it when, in reality, I was terrified, repulsed and in pain. These were the worst of times.

When my father had finished with me, he would warn me to keep quiet, often pushing me to the floor, then walking out and leaving me alone until my mother returned.

Although I hurt, it wasn't the physical pain or the sense of betrayal, abandonment or loneliness that gripped me. It was the conviction that I was dirty and guilty. I knew that what had gone on was wrong, and I was sure it was my fault and I was bad. I was desperate to clean and tidy everything up, as best I could as a child: myself, the furniture, the room … before my mother came home. I didn't want her to know, and be angry with me.

But as soon as she walked in she knew. She always kept the house immaculate, and she would notice anything out of place, or any trace of blood, or oil from my father's clothes that I had missed. Maybe she just saw the fear and guilt in my face. Whatever it was, she would look at me with eyes of contempt that seemed to pierce to the core of me, passing silent judgment.

It was the look I feared more than anything – the look that blamed me, not just for the abuse, but for being conceived, for being born, for being me. She told me repeatedly that she wished I'd never been born, and made it clear with tight-lipped, angry silences that I was incapable of pleasing her.

But on these occasions she didn't shout. Instead, almost under her breath, with hatred in her tone, she called me "wicked" and "dirty" and, pointing angrily at the bedroom, commanded, "Get in there." I was punished like a criminal imprisoned in a cell.

My Escape

But being shut away meant much more than being physically alone and isolated. I was carrying a massive burden of guilt and self-recrimination, and there was no outlet for emotion, no responsible adult to offer support or comfort, to lighten a load that was just too heavy for a child.

This is what had forced me to escape to the "nothing place," to mentally separate myself from the horror of the circumstances, to chop off, block out and leave behind the whole devastating experience. As a child, I don't think there was any other way I could have coped.

Desperation for Love

Although we grew up in the same home, I felt as if my brother got off lightly. My father didn't sexually abuse him, and my mother didn't have the same bitterness and anger in her heart towards him. Even so, in adult life, he has had his own problems, having served sentences in both young offenders' institutions and, later, in prison.

When he was small, my mother would pick him up and cuddle him. She didn't hate him, and he wasn't punished as often or as severely. I didn't like my brother. I was jealous of the attention my mother gave him, and I remember now wanting to lock him away in a cupboard. But I wouldn't have dared to do that, or to question my mother about what she said and did. In any case, it probably never occurred to me, because I didn't think she could be wrong.

In different ways, I was afraid of both my parents, but I desperately wanted their love, especially my mother's. With the naïve logic of a child, I believed I was born "bad," and was therefore guilty and to blame for everything that went wrong in my parents' lives. However much I wanted it, I judged myself undeserving of their love or anyone else's.

In working through these issues as an adult, I have learned that the injustice of being severely sexually abused and emotionally deprived in childhood, can be likened to an innocent man serving a lifetime's prison sentence in dire conditions. Ultimately, it becomes easier for him to believe he is guilty and deserves the punishment given than to live with the pain of the injustice.

For a child the pain and hopelessness of being "bad" and unloved, yet desperately longing for love, was potentially overwhelming. But I never stopped trying to "be good," believing that one day I would somehow wipe the guilty slate clean, and then my parents would love me and everything would be all right.

It was a hopeless fantasy, yet when my mother told me she wished I'd never been born, or I was the root of all her problems, or she wished she'd gone through with the adoption she had originally planned for me, her words just goaded me to try harder to please her.

Teenage Years

We moved house twice. When I was seven we moved from London to East Anglia, and at ten we moved down to the south of England. Even though each move was supposed to give us a "new start," nothing changed. Eventually, during my early teens, my father left us for another woman and my parents divorced and, for a while, I thought the abuse had stopped.

But he began to make regular visits to our home, taking me off in his car, often driving at high speeds to frighten me before reaching our destination. During my teenage years, his acts of humiliation and sexual defilement were the most extreme and the most distressing. But I continued to block out every horrific experience and do all I could to carry on with life as if it wasn't happening.

Leaving School

When I was in the sixth form, there was a time when I had to take several days off school, because I was in so much physical pain. I was anxious and stressed, but the focus of my anxiety was completely misplaced: I was fraught about school work because I was struggling to keep up.

I didn't have the support that others had, and had now taken time off. I was gripped by the fear of falling behind, perhaps not making the grade, failing and getting into trouble. As a result, while my mother was away for a few days, I went back to school, brought my belongings home and decided not to go back.

By the time my mother returned, I had taken up a job in a shop, one of a national chain of stores. It was a relief to be making a new start. I felt as if I was released from a past I didn't want to remember. In reality, I was leaving behind much more than I understood – not just school, but the traumatized part of myself that later became known as Sarah 16.

A New Beginning

I began my new job, feeling insecure and shrinking from attention, slipping into the staff room each morning hoping to be unnoticed. There was always plenty of chatter going on, and I would sit quietly, trying to be invisible, anxious to get down to the shop floor where I could throw myself into work. It was such a relief – to be able to lose myself in working hard.

The management team affirmed and encouraged me, and steadily I grew in confidence. I began to lift my head and dare to speak and join in conversations. I started to wear make-up and buy smart clothes with the money I was earning.

Little by little I was given more responsibility, and began to be asked to go and help at other branches of the company around the country, sometimes for a few days, sometimes a few weeks or months. I welcomed these opportunities to get away from home, to be independent and to shine at my job. Gradually I was promoted through the management ranks, moving to different branches until, eventually, I became the youngest store manager in the company.

I had a bright and promising new career, but behind the scenes I continued to live a sort of double life. I was striving to be like the people around me, to be "normal" and acceptable, on a professional level. Yet as soon as I left work to go home at night I became like an anxious child, fearful of my mother's control, worried about how to be and what to say to her. I was still a child desperate to avoid making her "cross" and to earn her approval.

It continued to be a very unstable environment. My father would still turn up without any warning to take me off in his car. And I was always on red alert for his "visits," although he never physically forced me to go with him. The truth is, he didn't have to. I was always so afraid of him he only had to look at me and I would do whatever he signaled. Sometimes he took me to his new home. Sometimes he drove me out into the countryside and the abuse took place in the car.

An End to Abuse

It finally stopped when I was eighteen. Through my career, I broke away from both my father's abuse and, at least circumstantially, my mother's domination and control. The company was accommodating me in hotels during my temporary stints of working in other branches, and then I rented a flat when I was promoted to a position in another town.

I was happier, stronger, an altogether more confident person. At the time I put this wholly down to my successful career. I couldn't connect with the true reason that it was such a relief to be away from home, because by then the extremity of my past had caused me to separate myself from it completely.

Coping without Memory

All the memories were hidden in my imprisoned, fragmented parts and, as an adult, I had no access to them, until the time many years later at Ellel Grange when all the parts eventually became united to the "adult me" as one whole person.

People often ask how I coped for so many years unable to access my childhood memories. The answer is that until I began to receive help, I didn't ever think about it. I never faced up to not being able to remember.

There was certain factual information I knew, like the addresses I'd lived at and the schools I'd attended, and I thought that was memory. When something came up that I should have been able to recall, and couldn't, I was just frustrated with myself. I didn't see it as a disability, but a failing. I was embarrassed and bluffed, but it didn't happen often because I became very good at sidestepping issues and steering conversations, so that I wouldn't have to expose my weakness.

Without realizing what I was doing, I held on to a false, idealized view of the past. It was as if I had brainwashed myself. And it worked until I reached that point in life where those parts who were buried inside and carried the truth, could no longer bear to be imprisoned and were pressing up, desperate to be heard and to be set free.

CHAPTER 7

Release from Psychiatric Care

In May 1997, I had an appointment with Dr Searle, which Fiona attended as well. It was a positive and encouraging time. Dr Searle said he was impressed by the changes he saw in me, so much so that he was prepared to release me from his care into the care of Ellel Ministries.

He said he had always known I "had eighteen years of vileness" and that I "came from a worse place than most." From the beginning of my time in hospital he had observed my irrational beliefs. He said the way he saw it, it was as if the walls of my life were held up by very thin wallpaper with nothing else behind it, and it would have been cruel for him to take "the wallpaper" down, because I would have collapsed and he couldn't have put me back together.

I believe he was saying that if the full truth of my brokenness and the abuse of my childhood had been exposed at the hospital, the pain of the injustice and the cruelty of my own parents could easily have tipped me over the edge.

It was only then that I really understood how it is that God alone can rebuild a shattered life. He had patiently revealed His unconditional acceptance, love and faithfulness, which had, ultimately, provided the strength for me to begin to let go of the crutches and face the painful realities of my life. He hadn't come at me with a bulldozer, but as the Master Craftsman, who was painstakingly rebuilding as He gently dismantled.

Dr Searle had always wanted to help me and had done his best, in prescribing medication designed to control the symptoms of fear and self-hatred, and the suicidal desires that came up from the broken parts inside.

During the first few months of my visits to Ellel Grange I was still taking very high dosages of antidepressants, tranquilizers and sleeping tablets, and there were times when I felt guilty that I wasn't wholly relying on God. But Dr Searle had encouraged me that it was as if I was in the middle of the sea trying to get to a rock (which I interpreted as The Rock!). He had said I wasn't strong enough to get there on my own, but the medication was keeping me afloat while I made progress. I had found this profoundly helpful.

Now at this meeting, fourteen months after the ten-day Healing Retreat, Fiona and I talked to him about the shattered parts of my personality. It felt right to allow Sarah 12 to the surface and, as the twelve-year-old, in whom I was by that time free and happy, I talked with Dr Searle. He understood the brokenness he was encountering, but said to Fiona, "The problem you will have is in integrating these parts." He was right. She couldn't do it, and nor could I or anyone else. It had to be a work of God, the Creator, putting me back together.

Five months after my first visit to Ellel Grange, I was free of all psychiatric medication and experiencing no withdrawal symptoms whatsoever. And now at this meeting, Dr Searle verified the healing I was receiving through prayer ministry and discharged me from the psychiatric hospital.

This was a wonderful milestone for me. It was over two years since I had first sunk down into depression and attempted to take my own life. I had been through a long time of believing I would never be free of psychiatric drugs and hospitalization, and this release was cause for celebration, despite the fact that we all knew there was more work to do.

CHAPTER 8

How Can I Forgive?

My fragmented parts had received tremendous healing. They were no longer in a traumatized, tormented state. Where there had been deep insecurity in each part, there was now a solid inner core of security that came from having released the pain of the past, and from knowing they were loved in the present, and from this they drew enormous strength. There were no more panic attacks or desperate suicidal longings surging forth from these parts. They had come to a place of peace and were ready to be joined together at the right time.

In the "adult me," there was relief, yet at the same time confusion and frustration: if they are all free and happy, why do I still struggle with the consequences of my past, and why does this process of healing have to take so long?

God gave one of my counselors some insight that was profoundly helpful. He said that there are different types of concrete: some that have all the right ingredients with no additives and develop increasing hardness over time, so are slow setting. And there are some that have chemicals added that make them develop strength quickly, so they are fast setting, but the problem with this type is that experiments show they don't endure.

God was saying He wasn't offering a "quick-fix" and bypassing unresolved issues, but developing His strength in me so that I would remain strong and endure. I realized He was answering my heart cry from the very beginning for "real healing." This meant a great deal to me, and I was strengthened to carry on.

Forgiving Myself

It was time to look at the issue of forgiveness again. During my very first visit to Ellel Grange, we had talked about the need to forgive both others and ourselves, but at that time, with no memory of my past, the only person I blamed and felt I perhaps needed to forgive was myself.

I was so full of guilt and shame, not just for being depressed and bulimic, but for being unable to sleep with John, for the stress he was under, for failing my children, for taking up my counselors' time ... Somehow I turned every situation around in my mind, so that even things that went wrong that, in fact, were nothing to do with me, felt as if they were my fault. I was angry and hated myself. This is what I wrote in my journal in those early days:

> *I need to forgive myself. All the guilt inside makes it very hard to do that. I blame and abuse myself, because I can't forgive myself, and the lack of forgiveness leads to suicidal thoughts. In my heart I am turning myself against myself.*

The journal goes on, telling of the overwhelming sense of guilt I felt because I couldn't forgive myself, and then the compulsive drive to punish myself by cutting my arms or even overdosing. Fiona and Anna urged me, "This isn't God's way," and encouraged me to pray. I told God that I wanted to forgive myself, because that was what the Bible said I should do, but it was hard and I needed His help.

Dealing with False Guilt

I had developed a lifestyle of blaming and punishing myself: starving myself of food, of love and anything that might be nice. As time went by and I was grasping the truth of my abusive past, God began to encourage me, through my counselors, not to just say sorry for all the self-accusation, but to choose actively to turn away from it.

False guilt was not only standing in the way of me recognizing where the guilt really belonged, but also robbing me of being able to receive and hold on to the positive that God was now bringing into my life. I constantly fed on negative comments, no matter how small they were in comparison to the positive, and even received anything that was given as a positive word in a negative light. If my counselors told me they thought I was doing well, and were happy to give me an afternoon to myself, I perceived it as, "I'm a horrible person ... They don't want to be with me ... They want to get away from me," etc.

This had become a lifetime's habit, and hard as it was, I gradually realized that I needed to work at resisting this false guilt that was so tormenting. The Bible says, "take captive every thought to make it obedient to Christ" (2 Corinthians 10:5), and "Hate what is evil; cling to what is good" (Romans 12:9).

Walking away from it and learning to dwell on the good and be kind and nurture myself was extremely hard and a journey in itself. It went so much against the grain of what I wanted to do. But because God was working at a deep level, revealing the abuse and the way I had internalized my emotions, I was able to understand why I behaved the way I did.

Fiona and Anna helped me to recognize that I had legitimate needs (including needs for love and food), and that it wasn't right to bat them down. I was aware of the Holy Spirit in me, witnessing to the truth of their words, and it was

Him who enabled me, step by step, to make hard choices to stop making myself sick and buying laxatives, to let go of the bulimia, and to allow myself to eat nice food and have treats. They were choices to yield to what God was showing me was a better way.

Forgiveness Detached from Pain

When it came to forgiving my parents, to begin with I didn't have a problem. I had lived my life by obeying rules, and my first thought wasn't that forgiveness was going to be hard, but that the Bible instructs us to forgive: "Forgive us our debts, as we also have forgiven our debtors ... But if you do not forgive men their sins, your Father will not forgive your sins" (Matthew 6:12, 15).

With mechanical obedience, I spoke out, "Dear Lord Jesus, I forgive my parents and release them into the freedom of my forgiveness." It wasn't that I didn't mean what I was saying. As much as I was able, my heart was in the words, but my emotions were completely buried.

Praying the prayer didn't bring any great sense of relief, and I began to understand that the problem was that not only were my emotions disconnected, but at the same time as forgiving, in my heart I was also still excusing my parents' behavior and going back to turning the blame back on myself: "They had a hard time with me. I wasn't an easy child." And I was denying and minimizing the effect of my parents' wrongdoing: "I'm OK. Even if my parents got some things wrong, it hasn't really affected me that much."

Slowly I realized that my forgiveness was incomplete, if it didn't involve more than a mental decision detached from pain. The forgiveness of my heart could only be true and complete if I made a choice to hand over the judgment of my parents to God, to fully release them, pardoning them for all they had done, whilst in the midst of feeling my own emotional responses to my past. This was going to be much harder. But this was the place God had brought me to.

Self-hatred Was My Defense

It was always easier to be angry with myself than with my parents or anyone else. But through counseling, I was grasping more and more not only the truth of the abuse but also the truth that while the hatred and venom inside was directed inwards, I was avoiding facing the fact that it was my parents' actions towards me that were bad, and that as a child I hadn't deserved to be abused.

God had already helped me to see that punishing myself wasn't right, and He wanted me to face the truth and the pain that I was denying. Speaking about God, the Bible says: "you desire truth in the inner parts" (Psalm 51:6).

And speaking about us:

"you will know the truth, and the truth will set you free."
(John 8:32)

I could see that being truthful with myself and God was the only way to real freedom, but I was full of fear.

The Festering Wound Uncovered

It was the Holy Spirit in me that began to help me to connect to and feel my true emotions. To my shock, I discovered there wasn't just pain inside me, but boiling anger at the injustice of what my parents had subjected me to, and there was bitterness, resentment and not only unforgiveness but a real desire for revenge. I had murderous feelings towards my parents; I hated what they had done to me, and I hated what they had withheld from me. I was jealous of what others had had that I hadn't. I had a deep heart cry of "I wanted it all to be different!" And I hated the way it had affected my whole life, and John and the children's lives.

The whole process was like having a dirty dressing taken off a deep festering wound. I knew I couldn't have walked through this on my own. It was something God enabled me to do, and through which He walked with me, as I will share in the next chapter.

Facing Up to How I Really Felt

Being brutally honest with myself and God in my struggle with all the negative emotions and the unforgiveness in my heart, was important. I needed to own the truth of how I really felt inside, which was devastating to me. To others it was totally understandable, but I had always tried so hard to be "good," and when I realized just how bitter, resentful and jealous of others I was, I felt so guilty. But I couldn't change it. This was me.

I was allowing God into the wound, and I could see that the next step on this journey meant releasing my pain to Him and, in the midst of feeling all my bitterness and unforgiveness, choosing to forgive my parents. But it was hard. When I was in touch with my feelings, I really didn't *want* to forgive. How could I forgive what seemed to me utterly unforgivable, and had damaged me so much?

I made angry protestations: "My life has been so messed up and yet, my Dad, who damaged me so much, is getting on with his life without any repercussions! Why has he got off free, while I'm left in such a mess? He's the one who should be suffering! Why should I forgive him? It's not fair!"

Testing and Checking

I vented my feelings and struggled. I was stubborn and argumentative, which was hard for Fiona and Anna, who were doing their very best to help me. My behavior in the counseling sessions was in stark contrast to the way I had been during my early visits to Ellel Grange, when I was completely passive.

But even then, because my trust had been so shattered when I was young, I had only ever trusted in my own ways of dealing with my problems (the chopping off and blocking out). Although I had bent over backwards to please people, I had never really trusted anyone. As my true feelings came to life, I couldn't just forgive, trusting this was the way to freedom because that was what my counselors told me.

In reality, the team were wholly trustworthy, yet I couldn't hand my trust over to them. It was even harder to trust in the God I couldn't see. I needed to work things through with them and Him, checking out for myself whatever counsel I was given, until I was sure it was a right and safe step to take.

God, in His mercy and grace, gave me the time I needed to work through, on the one hand, the pain and injustice of being abused and unloved and, on the other hand, the conviction that I needed to forgive, knowing that Jesus, wholly sinless, had cried out, "Father, forgive them" (Luke 23:34) when He was nailed to the cross. Eventually, through the enabling power of God's Holy Spirit, I was able to pray, "Lord, please will You help me to want to want to forgive."

What Does It Mean to Forgive?

I had to look at what it really meant to forgive. I thought it meant my parents would somehow be "let off," or that what I had gone through and what had taken such a long time for me to embrace would have to be forgotten, somehow pushed under the carpet again. If this was the case, I knew I couldn't do it. It was impossible.

But I discovered that, first of all, it didn't mean that my father or my mother would never have to answer for what they had done. I learned that it meant letting go of *my own judg-ment* on them, because it was too big for me. Yes, when I felt the raging emotions, I wanted to hurt them, I wanted them to hurt like I hurt, I wanted them to know what it felt like for me. But even if I had killed them, would that have made it all right? No! The only way was to hand the judgment over to God, so that one day they would have to answer to Him for their actions. Romans 12:19 says,

> Do not take revenge, my friends, but leave room for God's wrath, for it is written: "It is mine to avenge; I will repay," says the Lord.

I learned, too, that God was never going to ask me to "just forget it." He was going to heal the wounds, but when all my broken parts were finally joined together and I could look back down the years at all my memories, what happened to me was going to be very much part of who I am. Not that it was going to define me as a person, but from the reality of my childhood experiences would flow real compassion for others who have suffered similarly.

Unforgiveness: Like a Hidden Cancer

I began to see that the unforgiveness in my heart wasn't hurt-ing the people who had hurt me. The only person it was really damaging was me. It was eating away at me inside like a can-cer. It was a breeding ground for the bitterness, the resentment and the jealousy.

One day, when I was at home and John was at work and the children at school, a friend came to see me. When the front doorbell rang, I ran and hid in the bedroom, but she called through the letterbox, "Sarah, it's Jill. I know you're in there. Let's have a cup of coffee together." I couldn't ignore her and fearfully opened the door.

She hugged me and told me she loved me, and we sat and talked. I told her how difficult it was to forgive, and she shared with me that when she had gone through a traumatic time earlier in her life, soon after it happened, she knew she could allow the incident either to make her bitter, or better. She had a choice to make.

I knew the same choice was there for me. I could either remain unforgiving and bitter, continuing to keep myself in isolation, trying to avoid any situation that might touch into my pain and bring the anger and jealousy surging to the fore, or I could trust in God's promises of restoration.

I had been reading the story of Joseph in the Bible and saw that during all the years of unfair suffering in his life he denied bitterness taking root in his heart, and prayed and waited for God's restoration. Finally he was able to say to his brothers, who had sold him into slavery:

> "You intended to harm me, but God intended it for good to accomplish what is now being done, the saving of many lives."
> (Genesis 50:20)

I remembered, too, the promise of Romans 8:28:

> And we know that in all things God works for the good of those who love him, who have been called according to his purpose.

I wanted to make the choice to be better, to trust in God's promises of restoration and redemption.

But They Don't Deserve to Be Forgiven!

Forgiveness was the way forward. And, of all the reasons I should forgive, I knew the greatest was that I myself am forgiven. But I had to be honest with God and tell Him that what my father did to me seemed in my mind a far worse sin than anything I had ever done, and I couldn't see how he deserved to be forgiven.

Eventually, I learned that it wasn't about "deserving." I didn't deserve to be forgiven for the things I'd done wrong in my life, not least having ignored God completely for many years of my life. How would I have felt if my children had turned their backs on me?

The truth was that I didn't deserve to be rescued from the bottom of that deep dark pit I had been in; I didn't deserve to have this team of people standing around me, loving me, encouraging me, believing in me and believing in real freedom for me; I didn't deserve to have a husband who was standing firm in his love for me through times when many wouldn't have blamed him for walking away. I was being given so much that I didn't deserve.

It wasn't about getting what was due. It was about love – God's love. It was God's love that had brought every good thing into my life, none of which I had any special right to.

I thought about this same love that had motivated God to send Jesus to die on the cross. Not only did Jesus take the punishment for my sin so that I could be forgiven, but in suffering all the pain and anguish of the cross, being stripped naked, enduring nails being hammered into his hands and feet, and being mocked and jeered at, He had chosen to identify Himself with my suffering. And He had chosen to take my wounds and pain upon Himself, so that I could be healed and set free.

Walking this path to healing was about choosing to accept by faith His sacrifice for me in a very real way, and it was about willingly following Jesus' example. Even as He hung on the cross, dying in agony, He cried out, "Father, forgive them, for they do not know what they are doing" (Luke 23:34).

Not by Might Nor by Power, But by My Spirit ...

Finally, I had reached the place where I *wanted* to forgive, but I knew I was incapable of forgiving in the way Jesus did. Alexander Pope famously wrote, "To err is human, to forgive is divine." I needed God's help.

I prayed, "Lord, please will You help me to freely forgive my parents in the same way You forgave when You, who had never done anything wrong, were abused in the worst possible way, even to the point of death."

Since that time, day by day, His Holy Spirit has been working in me, changing me, giving me a willing heart to forgive. It hasn't been something He has just landed on me, but each time I have felt the pain and injustice, I have cried out to Him afresh, asking Him to help me to forgive. And, little by little, I know He has been enabling me.

Even with God's help, it would have been impossible for me to forgive once and for all time. Forgiveness had to become a lifestyle that I learned to develop, and am still learning to develop. No wonder Jesus said we should forgive "not seven times, but seventy-seven times" (Matthew 18:22).

I am so grateful that neither God nor my counselors forced me to forgive. They didn't say, "As a Christian, you *have* to forgive" or, "We can't help you anymore until you've forgiven." So much was forced on me in my childhood, and I was robbed of making choices for myself. It meant a lot that I was given the time I needed to get to the place where I was ready to forgive, in the reality of all that my parenting had cost me and my family, for the simple reason that I truly *wanted* God's way, more than I wanted to hold on to my unforgiveness. And, although it has been hard, I have felt a deep joy inside as the Holy Spirit has enabled me to choose God's way and say "no" to mine.

My Mother's Death

I would have loved to have been reconciled with my mother. The biggest pain in my life was that she never loved me.

However, even though she continued to work as John's secretary and I had become so unwell, she never relented in refusing to talk to John about anything on a personal level, either regarding herself or us. Eventually she became sick and was away from work for an extended period. All John knew was that she had a cough. I wrote to her telling her I was sorry to hear she was ill. I didn't receive a reply.

While I was at Ellel Grange, John heard from his colleagues that she had undergone an operation for cancer and was at home recovering. He went to visit her, taking flowers and magazines, but even then she stood firm in refusing to enter into any conversation, other than telling him when she might expect to be back at work.

Some time later, my brother, who neither John nor I had seen for many years, walked into John's office and told him that my mother had passed away, and that her dying wish, which she had written into her will, was that John and I were not to be made welcome at her funeral.

Forgiveness had opened the door of the prison of bitterness I was in. Sadly, my mother, as far as I know, never knew that freedom.

CHAPTER 9

Pain, Anger and Bitterness

During my ongoing visits to Ellel Grange, as I was letting go of denial, allowing the truth to stand and working towards forgiving, I felt as if I was opening a door behind which was pain. It stood like a great, heavy wardrobe. And I had such a fear that if I dared to really look at it, it would come crashing down on top of me, and I would be crushed beneath it.

Recognizing that God intends every child to be loved and cherished by their parents, but that I had been hated and rejected, and that the hands that should have held me safely, had stolen my innocence and beaten me, was hard to face. So often, I wanted to shut that half-open door and run away from it.

But I had been allowing my pretense to be stripped away (the strong, capable exterior), and God was bringing my emotions to life. Inside, where He intended there to be a solid core of personal worth and value that comes from a life built on a foundation of love, I could feel a great chasm of emptiness. There wasn't a strong inner core, but instead an intense craving for something or someone to come and fill this empty place. I was beginning to feel the injustice, the pain, the anger and the loss.

Until the time when I began to work through forgiving my parents, the emotions I had been expressing had come out of my responses to present-day situations, like the anger I felt when my counselors had first begun to demonstrate love to me, or the fear when I was at home alone and felt abandoned, or the panic that rose up whenever I felt out of control. I always felt as if my emotions were related to the now. But God was beginning to show me that it was my responses to the past that fuelled such strong responses in the present.

The Pain of the Legacy

Mixed in with this was the pain of the legacy of my past. It hurt that I wanted to be mothered as an adult *now*. It hurt that my head had been so messed up. I didn't want to have been in a psychiatric unit. I didn't want even the thought of physical intimacy with my husband to be dirty and detestable to me. It was painful that I had unavoidably hurt John so much, and that my children had suffered through having such a dysfunctional, obsessive mother.

Self-harm – An Escape Path

Fiona and Anna encouraged me, in the adult place, to face the painful reality and to learn to process my emotions in a healthy way, just as all my fragmented parts had done. But whenever I felt we were getting anywhere near touching the emotional pain, I had a driving compulsion to self-harm. I would suddenly start punching my legs violently or driving my thumbnail backwards and forwards across my wrist until it bled, or dive out of the room into my bedroom, intent on finding a mirror or something I could cut myself with. Physical pain pushed away the emotional pain that I was so afraid of.

Over time, I learned to stop in my tracks and tell my counselors when I wanted to escape by self-harming. With gentle sensitivity, but with firmness, they helped me to see that, however hard and painful it was, there was always a choice to be made. I could face the issues, looking to God and them to help me, or I could keep running down my well-worn escape paths.

It's Too Big!

I wanted to make good choices, but it was hard. I struggled many times. Sometimes I would try to divert the conversation, or switch off by turning my attention to systematically tidying the room.

But eventually, as I yielded to God's Spirit in me, I began to ask Fiona and Anna, "How do I give the pain to Jesus? How do you *do* that?" They encouraged me to get it *out*, instead of keeping it all locked up inside me – to talk it out, cry it out, stamp my feet, kick a ball, rip up a phone book, punch a cushion ... I was even offered the use of a tree at Ellel Grange that has very soft bark that can withstand being punched, without causing grazed knuckles. I gave it a try, but somehow it wasn't enough. "What's in me is explosive!" I railed. "It's much bigger than that!"

As I got in touch with my feelings I really didn't feel safe. I wanted to smash up the room I was in. I wanted to go out and kill someone, and even that didn't feel as if it would be enough. It was true that the pain inside me was big. But it was also true that the fear of unleashing it was even bigger.

The Power of Prayer

The Ellel teaching had helped me to understand that there are powers of darkness at work in the world that are opposed to the ways of God. I recognized how they operate through human beings to accomplish the horrific things we read about in the newspapers every day: the acts of terrorism, torture, murder and child abuse.

The team pointed out that these powers of evil weren't giving up in their attempts to ruin my life without a fight.

They wanted to keep me locked into the consequences of abuse, and were whispering lies into my ears: Jesus' sacrifice on the cross wasn't big enough for my pain; I would always be tormented; I would never be able to walk free and live life as a normal human being.

I learned that it was important to make a stand against the lies, countering them with the truth I believed: that God had promised to heal me and He *was going to keep His promise*! As I spoke out these words of truth, my counselors prayed for God to hold back the dark forces.

The voices were silenced, and the anguish and sense of hopelessness abated. Until I had begun to receive help from Ellel, I had never understood the amazing power of prayer over the powers of darkness.

Getting the Mess Out

I was left with some fears, but not the same gripping fear as before. One of my fears was that the pain *was* me, and that if I let go of it there wouldn't be anything left, just a shell, a kind of non-person.

Another was that my emotions were "bad," and that they weren't going to come out nicely. I knew there was so much more than tears that needed to be released. "What if what's in me is really bad? What if I lose control and do something terrible?" I asked. Fiona and Anna encouraged me that I didn't need to worry, because God already knew what was inside me: it wasn't going to shock Him. And I saw that they weren't afraid either, because they trusted that God was going to be in control.

Eventually, resisting all my escape paths, I allowed what had been so pressed down to begin to come out. It was hard and painful. I cried and shouted, punched cushions, hit the floor, made angry accusations, spoke out how much I hated what my parents had done, and desperately questioned, "Can

God wipe away the tears? Can He restore the years the locusts have eaten?" (see Joel 2:25).

God wasn't shocked, but I was! It was so messy, so explosive, so heartfelt. It didn't come out neatly and it wasn't all pain. There was bitterness, hatred and resentment. "Does this mean I really am a bad person?" I pleaded. "No, no," Fiona responded, "it doesn't mean you're bad. These are normal emotions."

I began to grasp that I didn't have to clean myself up for God. He had sent Jesus down into the mess of this world, and He wasn't critical or disapproving of the mess that was inside me. In reality, He was all-compassionate and wanted me to allow Him to comfort me in my mess.

From Denial to Self-pity

Having begun to express my feelings and finding that the release brought relief, I continued. But instead of receiving God's comfort, I swung from denial to the opposite extreme, the extreme of self-pity, which fed all my negative emotions: the anger, bitterness, resentment and jealousy.

I wanted others, especially my counselors, to feel how I felt, and sometimes I went far beyond healthily expressing pain, to venting my emotions with real venom and sarcasm, in attempts to "show them what it's like for me." There were even times when I wasn't simply venting my anger, with them alongside, but I was venting my anger *at* them instead. I was projecting what, in reality, I felt about my mother onto them: "You don't care about me! You've got your own lives. I'm just your job!"

This was not only intensely unfair on them, but I came to learn that it doesn't matter how much we want someone else to know how we feel, no other human being can feel our feelings. Others can come alongside and empathize and offer comfort and care, but our feelings are unique to us. God is the only One who knows exactly how we feel.

Confronting My Sin

Getting to the place of expressing my true feelings about the injustice of my past was a sign of good, healthy progress. God, through the team, had allowed me to shout and remonstrate. I had lived in far too much fear of punishment to be free to vent my anger as a child. Being given the freedom to express such things as, "I hate my dad!" and even, "I hate *you!*", and to find that God and my counselors hadn't rejected me, but were still there for me, helped me grow in learning to trust.

I learned that God wasn't like my earthly father: He wasn't going to beat me for expressing my feelings. In fact, He was the opposite. He cared. And little by little I discovered that He, too, was angry at what my parents had done to me.

But the problem was that I didn't want to let go of my negative emotion. I wanted to keep on expressing it, and I was directing it at my counselors. So, there came a point where Fiona knew she had to confront me, saying, "Sarah, this is sin!"

This provoked a very angry response in me. For a long time, the team had been doing all they could to encourage me to trust in love. They had nurtured me, held me, laughed and cried with me, and shown me all the passages in the Bible that spoke of God's amazing love for me. It had felt as if they were coaxing me to stand in the middle of a rug on the floor, but I was so afraid that if I did, it would be pulled out from under my feet, and I would go flying. But, eventually, I did trust in the love they showed me, and now as Fiona's words rang in my ears, I felt as if the very thing I had feared had come to fruition – the rug had been pulled out, and I had been badly hurt in the process.

Infuriated, I shouted, "I came here believing I was bad! And now you're telling me I *am* bad!" Being confronted had catapulted me back to a place of fear – the huge fear of being bad, and of being punished. This was one of the fears that had dominated me throughout my childhood.

It's OK to be Bad!

Fiona and Anna helped me to work through the confusion, and to see that this fear didn't have to continue to control me forever – not because I was suddenly going to somehow be perfect and never have to worry about being bad again! That would be impossible. But because, just like every other human being, I had times when I was "bad," when I got things wrong, but it was all right, because God had sent Jesus to pay the penalty for us all. I just needed to receive His forgiveness.

Although I had found it very hard to be faced up with my sin, I slowly grasped the truth that we all sin, and there are times when we all need others to help us see it, because we are all so much better at seeing other people's sin than our own! Jesus described it as "having planks in our eyes" (see Matthew 7:3-5). I learned that correction is as much a part of love as encouragement and affirmation. Proverbs 3:11-12 says,

> My son, do not despise the Lord's discipline and do not resent his rebuke, because the Lord disciplines those he loves, as a father the son he delights in.

The Infected Matter around the Wound

It was a very important part of my journey to healing. I was learning that my pain was important to God, but so was the way I dealt with it.

He wanted me to learn to bring the pain to Him so that He could comfort me and heal the wounds, but He wanted me to be willing to let go of my sin, the bitterness and resentment, which was like infected matter around the wound.

He knew I couldn't let go of it by my own efforts. I couldn't change what had grown in my heart over a lifetime, but He wasn't expecting me to. He was simply asking whether I agreed with Him that this bitterness was unhealthy, and whether I *wanted* to let go of it. I said "Yes." And the Bible says,

> If we confess our sins, he is faithful and just and will forgive us
> our sins and *purify us from all unrighteousness.*
>
> > (1 John 1:9, my emphasis)

With my willingness, by the power of His Holy Spirit *He* was
going to do the work of cleansing the wound, changing in me
what I couldn't change.

What Does "Taking Pain to the Cross" Mean?

It had taken a long time to get to the place of releasing my
pain healthily, and as I was crying it out, I was also asking, "Is
this what 'taking pain to the cross' means? Does it mean getting it all from inside to outside? Does it mean just letting it all
go?" Abuse had cost me a lot, and I was afraid that somehow
my pain was just being discarded, that it had no value.

Gradually God helped me to see that by no means was He
rubbishing my pain. He wasn't saying it didn't count for anything. He showed me that when Jesus suffered and died on the
cross, He *validated* my pain. He chose to walk that path: yes,
because that's how much the cruel things that happen in our
lives matter to Him; yet even more, so that we can be healed
of the consequences of those things. Isaiah 53:5 says, "by his
wounds we are healed." Jesus knew the cost, and He alone
paid the ultimate price.

Finding Something Greater than My Pain

A divine transaction began to take place. As I cried my pain
out to God, He began to share His heart with me. Sometimes
He spoke through one of my counselors and at other times, as
my sensitivity to the voice of the Holy Spirit in me was growing, I just knew in my own heart what He was saying.

There were times when I would tell Him that I felt as if
I had lost everything, and He would gently speak back to me

that He *is* everything and that I have Him. He would remind me that He made me, He is my Creator and He owns the cattle on a thousand hills (Psalm 50:10). He would tell me that I am His daughter, and that everything He has is mine, and He wants to share it all with me. He would remind me that I have *His* inheritance.

He told me that those who have lost much can understand Him, because He lost so much too: He wasn't loved, He was hurt and even killed. He said that some people think they have everything, but they have *nothing*, because they don't have Him. "You have everything," He said, "because you have Me. I have even prepared a place for you in heaven, and here on earth I will never ever leave you. When you call to Me, I will answer. When you turn to the right or left, I'll say, 'This is the way.' You can give Me all your fears. I will comfort and love you. I will delight over you. I want to share My heart with you and want you to share your heart with Me. I want to give you special love for those who have nothing, because they don't have Jesus. When you feel your pain, remember My pain for all the children I have lost. Will you go and seek them? Sarah, will you find them and bring them to the sheepfold?"

These were the most precious of times, when the intensity of the pain and struggle began to dissipate, because I had found the real treasure that my heart had always longed for. It is this treasure that has stayed with me and that has motivated me to write this book.

I could see that *this* is where real healing is, not just for me, but for every person on the face of the earth, no matter what they have gone through in their lives. It's not that our losses disappear, but when we turn to God in the reality of our pain, He opens His arms to us and offers such love, such peace and such hope. It transcends all the losses.

Ongoing Dissociative Lifestyle

There were still one or two more hurdles I needed to get over. I no longer had a problem connecting to my emotions during my visits to Ellel Grange, when Fiona and Anna were with me. Sometimes I was tempted to grab back my old coping mechanisms of self-harming or obsessively cleaning and tidying but, in the main, I continued to release pain healthily. However, as soon as my counselors left to go home at night, it was as if a switch went off and my emotions disappeared.

It was the same whenever the time was approaching for me to leave to go home. And when I was at home, my feelings were completely blocked off and the Obsessive Compulsive Disorder had as strong a grip on me as it had ever had.

God showed me that there was a valley I needed to walk through on my own with Him. Ever since my first visit to Ellel Grange, I had always had Fiona and Anna by my side as I faced the issues of my past. I didn't want to face something hard without them. It was a very fearful prospect, but in my panic God, in His grace, highlighted this Bible verse to me,

> "Who is this coming up from the wilderness, leaning upon her Beloved?"
>
> (Song of Songs 8:5 NKJV)

I realized this meant I would have to walk through a difficult time, perhaps facing the reality of my life at a deeper level, but God was promising me that I would come through to the other side of it, free of the temptations to self-harm or obsessively clean and tidy my environment. I would no longer be looking for escape routes or needing counselors to support me, because I would truly know Him as my support for life.

God was leaving no stone unturned and was putting His finger on both my ongoing dissociative practice and the attachment disorder I had developed. I share how He brought me through these very real issues that were blocking the way to full healing for me in the remainder of the book.

The Place of Comfort Today

There are still times when I find myself in situations that touch into the pain of my past. I feel the pain and, because of that, some people would question my healing. But my answer to this is that my past played a very real part in shaping the person I am, and it is unrealistic to think it shouldn't hurt anymore. The difference today is that it no longer has any power over me.

Eventually, I walked through that valley with God, and I truly received *His* comfort in the place of pain. For a time, I had looked to people to empathize with me in my pain, but the comfort I found in God was on another level. And when I feel the pain today, He is the One I go to for comfort, the One who knows exactly where I have come from, and where He is taking me to. There is no love like His.

On my wall at home I have a picture of Jesus tenderly holding a lamb in His arms. He holds the lamb close to His heart with nail-pierced hands. This picture speaks to me time and time again. Jesus hasn't just picked up the lamb to pat it and say, "There, there!" The nail marks remind me that He was nailed to the cross to bear our sorrow and grief (Isaiah 53:5). He gave His all for us.

And then He rose to life again. He offers more than comfort. As He holds the lamb close, He imparts His new life into it, and our part is to receive His comfort and, with the strength this gives, to live the redeemed life He won for us to the full. John 10:10 says,

> *"The thief comes only to steal and kill and destroy; I have come that they may have life, and have it to the full."*

Chapter 10

God Finds Me!

From the very beginning it was always crucial to me to know that I was moving forward in my journey to healing. Though the struggles were intense at times, deep down there was real comfort in knowing that things were changing. The difficulty I had was that very often I couldn't assimilate the changes for myself. I would frequently need either John or one of my counselors to help me see the progress I was making.

I knew that seven fragmented parts had been rescued and were now healed. I was no longer getting the surges for suicide from them, but because I wasn't yet joined to them I couldn't sense their newfound strength and joy.

When I was at home, I knew that during the times I had spent at Ellel Grange I had expressed a great deal of pain and anger at the injustice of my past, but at home it all seemed very far removed from me. I was entrenched in making long lists of jobs and obsessively cleaning and tidying the house. Somehow I couldn't "connect" to whatever had happened in Lancaster. "I don't think I need to go back," I would say to John, "I think I'm all right now."

Of course, in reality, I wasn't. I was still highly controlled and unable to be spontaneous. We were still sleeping in separate bedrooms, and I still wasn't mixing with other people. "I like things tidy, and I like being on my own. There's nothing wrong with that!" I told myself.

Give Me the Plan

At Ellel Grange I always wanted to know what the plan was for the day, and as soon as I understood what we were dealing with, whether we were looking at my thoughts and beliefs or addressing the issue of forgiveness or pain, I worked at the agenda. Even though the issues were often difficult to face and it was a battle to follow them through, there was a safety for me in having a plan to work to.

Who Is This Person?

Fiona and Anna began to see that there was never anything of my own persona coming forth. If they said they liked the dinner, I liked it too, and if they didn't, neither did I. If one of them said they liked a particular color, I liked that color too. In reality, I couldn't express my own opinions and choices, because I didn't know what I liked or disliked, wanted or didn't want.

Most people begin to work out these things from very early on in life, but for those who come from an abusive background, childhood is about survival, not adventure and discovery.

One day I was sitting with four counselors and they began to discuss the question, "If you could do anything, what would you like to do?" At times like this I felt uncomfortable. And I was irritated because we weren't sticking to the plan!

One of the counselors, Jeremy, said with great excitement, "I'd love to ride a jet-ski!" I was completely taken aback and couldn't understand at all why he would want to do that. He turned to me and asked, "What would you like to do?" With some sense of self-righteousness, I said, "I want to get better, so I can help other people."

I know now that there is nothing wrong with having a heart to help others, but the fact is, I was trying to find my personal worth and value in "walking the path to healing" and then "helping others."

A Human Doing or a Human Being?

In my efforts to try and make sense of life I had learned to mimic others, and made life a treadmill of jobs to be endlessly worked at. Like many people, I was looking for my identity in "doing," and had never found the joy of simply "being."

God, the Creator, had made me to be a person in my own right, with my own unique identity, with all my own likes and dislikes, abilities and gifting, but I had only developed in my intellect. I could reckon and reason ad infinitum, and convince myself that black was white if necessary. I just thought that was how I was. I had never even thought that hidden inside me were many other God-given characteristics.

Some of them, like the enjoyment of music, were locked in my broken parts, but there was much in the "adult me" that I was completely unaware of, that had been crushed down inside.

Bad at the Core

Although I found it frustrating not having my own opinions like other people, I was afraid of looking too deeply inside myself. It was true I was growing in my sense of worth and value to God, and learning to walk out of the lifestyle of blaming and punishing myself, yet I still held the same rock-solid conviction that somewhere deep down inside I was bad, and I was afraid of this being exposed. Dealing with my fragmented parts had been different, because they were separate, but I didn't want to uncover what was at the heart of *me*.

I thought of myself like a bad apple that looked OK on the outside, but was rotten at the core. And during my early visits to Ellel Grange, when I had experienced that bitter conflict of wanting love yet hating love, and felt those terrible childlike yearnings to grab and snatch every bit of love and kindness I could get, it had confirmed to me that I was bad inside.

Some people describe themselves as having "an inner child." I believed I had a very *bad* inner child. It raged at the injustice of never being loved; it hated my parents and wanted to hit out in retaliation, not just at them, but at anyone. It wasn't that, as an adult, I didn't understand these feelings. In the counseling setting, I had worked them through myself. But I knew my inner child wanted to hold onto them and, worst of all, wanted to use others to satisfy her selfish, insatiable cravings.

It was like having a putrid wound that I was desperate to keep hidden. I couldn't bear the thought of anyone seeing it because, just as the pus from a festering wound reeks, so the attitudes that smoldered in this inner child were repulsive and shameful. At least this was how it seemed to me.

And because of this, all my concentration and energy was channeled into keeping this inner child separate and buried. It was my survival strategy. It was why I had turned my life into an endless list of jobs to be worked at, why I had become my own harsh taskmaster, and why I held so tightly to the agendas during the counseling sessions. I didn't want to let go of control.

Let Me Be Me!

It was around this time, when I was wading through the agenda for the day with Fiona, Anna and another member of the counseling team, Karen, that I began to feel an intense frustration with the whole process I was walking through. This was not a normal feeling for me. Knowing I was "dealing with the issues and sticking to the plan" had always given me a sense of security.

But at that particular instant, I felt very angry at facing yet another issue and, suddenly, from somewhere deep down inside, out of my mouth shot the words, "I'm not a machine! I'm a person!"

I shocked myself as well as my counselors, but this was a critical moment of truth. I had worked so hard all my life to override the "bad child" inside me, and suddenly *she* had over-ridden *me* and effectively cried out, "Let me be me!"

I didn't understand that this was what God wanted too. He wanted me to be free to be who I was inside. Ephesians 2:10 says,

> For we are God's workmanship, created in Christ Jesus to do good works, which God prepared in advance for us to do.

I had tried so hard to be "a good person," to be what I thought I should be, but I hadn't understood that that was *my work-manship*. God wanted me to let go of all the striving, even the striving to work at dealing with the consequences of my past, so that what *He had made, His workmanship*, the core of me, that He didn't see as bad but crushed and damaged, was allowed to come forth, just as I am.

As my counselors tried to explain this, my heart sank. Did this mean, then, that all the work we had done thus far was null and void, because it had all been done through the part of me that had tried so hard to be good and get it right?

Patiently, Fiona reminded me that the truth of my past had been exposed, my fragmented parts had been rescued and lovingly restored, and God had brought connection to my emotions for me as the "adult" at appropriate times, so that I could work through a lot of forgiveness and pain. I had struggled against my natural instincts to yield to God's way and allow the Holy Spirit to begin to melt the bitterness that had festered in my heart; and He wasn't now saying that because "Good Me" had always been intent on overriding "Bad Me," everything thus far had been false.

What He was saying was that, through fear, I had been like a tightly closed shell, and inside the shell was a beautiful pearl that had been badly damaged, and it was His time for the shell to gently open up, and for the pearl to be exposed and restored.

Matthew 13:45-46 says,

> "The kingdom of heaven is like a merchant looking for fine pearls. When he found one of great value, he went away and sold everything he had and bought it."

I couldn't get past seeing the core of my being, that inner child, as "bad," because I knew what was in there. And in my mind, it was only fit for annihilation. But God was saying I was so valuable to Him at the core that He had given up *everything* for me, even to death on the cross. And He was waiting for the time when I would trust Him enough to allow Him to reach down with His love, into that part I hated.

An Emotionally Under-developed Inner Core

From that point on, through my counselors, God began to encourage me to allow the shell to open and the "pearl" to be exposed.

"Don't try and work things out in your head," Fiona and Anna gently coaxed me. "Just listen to what's going on deep down inside. What's the heart cry that's bursting to be heard?"

I felt intensely angry, but underneath the anger was fear. I was like a rabbit caught in the headlights of a car: panic-stricken and desperate for somewhere to run. Despite having had that one defining moment of "wanting to be me," the thought of "connecting" to the longings of my heart was totally abhorrent. "You don't realize what's in there!" I railed at my counselors. I couldn't be convinced that what was pushing to come out wasn't bad, pathetic, shameful and embarrassing.

I battled with holding on to my lifetime's survival strategy of separation and yielding to God's way. Eventually, as the team prayed, I made a choice to say sorry to God for trusting my own way of coping, instead of trusting Him with *all* that I am. But separation had become a firmly entrenched way of life and I couldn't instantly let go of it and connect to the child within. Fearfully I asked God, by the power of His Holy Spirit, to bring the connection.

And as He did, I found myself crying out, with real heartache and the simplicity of a child, "I just want to be loved." The intense neediness in me had rushed to the fore, as it had done in the past. There was that same desperation to be held and hugged, for someone to look into my eyes and see the "inner child," to know me and want me. I was hungry to be nurtured as a little child.

These were the feelings from my childhood, when I had tried and tried to "be good" and please my mother, so that "in a minute she'll love me." That was how I had lived as a child, waiting and waiting for a touch, a smile, some expression of love from my mother that, ultimately, never came.

At that moment with my counselors, I was so immature and childlike that this "inner core" could easily have been mistaken for another fragmented part. But it wasn't another part that had broken away in an extreme moment of traumatic sexual abuse. It was the reality of how I was, as an adult, deep down inside, as a consequence of my childhood. It became clear that although my mind was highly tuned, inside I was a completely emotionally under-developed, insecure little girl.

I didn't see myself with compassion, but found it intensely embarrassing and shameful. I knew a few hugs weren't going to satisfy this "child." She would demand more and more and more. And, as far as I could see, she didn't want God, she just wanted to *use* people.

I hated her, and renewed my determination not to allow her to be seen again. I got myself together as a "sensible adult," bulldozing over, shutting down and separating myself from the child within. I pushed her out of my mind.

Learning to "Just Be"!

My counselors knew, however, that it was the inner child that
God wanted to reach and help, so that I could develop and
grow emotionally, and my fragmented parts could then be
joined to the "adult me," and I would be able to function prop-
erly as a "whole adult." This had always been the goal. The
team began to use creative activities to work at bypassing my
intellect and reaching the desperate place in me.

But I had so separated myself from it that I couldn't understand at all why we needed to "play." It felt like a waste of
precious time. I thought we should be working at belief sys-
tems and mindsets, or defense mechanisms, or emotions ...

"Sarah," Fiona said, "your greatest need is in your humanity. You need to learn to allow the 'real you' out, and 'just be'!"
I couldn't see what she meant and responded in frustration
with, "OK, but what shall I do, while I 'be'?!"

On one particular occasion, four counselors sat around me
with a pile of old seashells and a selection of brightly colored
paints, sequins and beads. "Let's have a go at painting and deco-
rating these shells," one of them said enthusiastically. Reluctantly
I joined in, thinking to myself, "This is the way a person is supposed to 'be,' so this is how I must work at 'being'!" I wasn't
connected to the fact that I had an emotional need deep down
inside. But I did feel threatened when they began to ask one
another, "Which color do you like?", because other than copying someone else's answer, I didn't know what to say.

The team didn't give up and, another time, we painted
the palms of our hands and made hand prints on paper. I was
going through the motions, but Fiona, Anna and Karen were
praying for God to help me to connect to my inner child.

Suddenly, as I lifted my wet, yellow-painted hand off the
paper, I began to laugh. But for the first time, this response
hadn't come from copying one of the others. This had come
right up from the inner child. It was a sign that, during that

short time, my barriers had come down, and the immature place inside was coming to life through the creative activities. This was a very significant and important moment.

Neediness v. Self-reliance

But I hated feeling like a needy child whilst trying to live as an adult, so I continued to push away and deny that immature part of me, and with it all the anger, shame, guilt and deep mistrust that was locked in it.

Trying to override and deny my inner self didn't, however, solve the problem. It just meant I had two extremes operating simultaneously:

- **Extreme neediness** coming from inside, which my counselors repeatedly told me was not "bad" but was the emotionally needy little girl in me, to whom God wanted to bring His comfort, strength and healing.

- **Extreme self-reliance** coming from "Good Me," from which place I would often say, "I don't know why I need help. I'm not going to let my past affect me anymore. I'm fine."

As the inner child was coming to life, the drive in "Good Me" to "fix" everything and make everything all right was still running, and my solution to the problem of the simultaneous extremes was a desire to live in either one of the extremes, and to chop off, block out and deny the other.

Much of the time, particularly when I was at home and away from my counselors, I completely forgot that part of me was in desperate emotional need. I worked at being "Good Me," a responsible, independent adult. In my rational mind, this made sense. I argued that it wasn't fair on my family for me "to have an immature childlike core." They needed me to be a fully functioning adult.

**The outer person fighting for survival
and the emotionally under-developed
core (the pearl)**

- Wants love (needs love)
- Hurts
- Afraid of being hurt again
- Wants to use others to get
  its needs met

Negative emotions respond from
the inner core to many present-day
situations, because of the injustice
of the past.

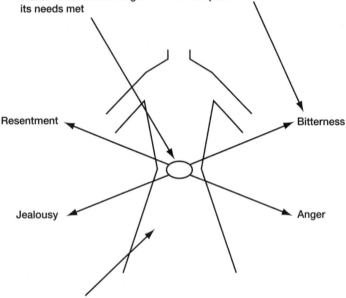

Resentment

Bitterness

Jealousy

Anger

**Person living everyday life fights
for survival (but it becomes a fight
against self)**

- Wants to be a "good person"
- Believes the "inner child" makes
  me a "bad person" (a negative,
  non-productive, draining,
  dependent person)
- Wants to be free of the hurting
  "inner child" because it causes
  so many difficulties
- Hates the negative emotions, the
  dependency and the need
- Wants to enter into fullness of life
- Wants "normality"

Copes by:

- Denial of "inner child"
- Lifestyle of "chopping off"
  and "blocking out"

Opposing agendas co-exist,
e.g. plan to self-harm/escape
by suicide, alongside desire to
trust God whatever the cost.

Figure 7.

Equally, there were other times when I was at Ellel Grange and would grasp that the inner child wasn't bad but needy and hurting, and then I wanted to abdicate my personal responsibility as an adult completely and "just be a needy child," wholly dependent on my counselors.

At these times, Fiona and Anna, and by then others who had joined the team, reminded me of the reality of my life at home: that I am married with children and rightful responsibilities. They were trying to help me recognize that just as the "inner child" wasn't false, neither was the adult, who was living everyday life, a completely false, unreal persona.

Finding Myself through Relationship and Creativity

My heart cry from the very beginning had been, "I want to be the same on the inside as I am on the outside." Through the traumas in my life, I had never found myself, never really knew who I was. But, through the help I was receiving, I was learning that I had never been lost to God.

He had been dismantling what was false in my life: the masks and the pretense; and through relationship and creative activities He was getting past my intellect and doing His work of reaching right down to the child within, putting back in what was missing in my life so that I could begin to develop and grow emotionally.

I had never bonded with my mother and, although as an adult my social skills had survived relatively intact, I did find relationships difficult. I was always desperate for other people's acceptance and approval, and couldn't stop myself working to earn it. At the same time I had never allowed anyone near my inner core, the inner child, where the very real responses to my past were locked: the neediness, shame, guilt, deep mistrust and fear of being hurt again.

Fiona and Anna began to take me for outings in the car. We would drive out to the countryside and go for walks or to the beach. On one occasion, I ran along a deserted beach with my arms stretched out, shouting, "I want to be me!" with Fiona and Anna following on behind! Despite my fears and struggles, the Holy Spirit was at work and what was inside was coming out!

As Fiona and Anna taught me the songs they had sung at Sunday School when they were children and as, in a very childlike way, I allowed myself to scribble with paints on paper with them, God was getting under my defenses and I learned to play. And as we played we laughed. And in the most natural way, the little girl in me was bonding with Fiona and Anna. Through creativity, from this crushed and denied core, I was learning about relationship; I was learning to "just be" with others, without working at earning their acceptance, or trying to achieve something. This was a miracle!

I began to learn about myself, too, for the very first time: I discovered the colors I liked and those I didn't. I discovered that I could be creative.

One evening after I had been with my counselors all day, I started to make a card for them to say "thank-you." Until that time, I had never made anything creatively, let alone to give to anyone else. I didn't think it was in me, and I would only have undertaken something like this as a serious job to be worked at. But it was fun! I enjoyed choosing the colors of the beads and the ribbons I stuck on the card, and when I had finished it I liked it and couldn't wait to give it to them!

I was discovering something that had always been in me but I had never found before, and I was learning to be spontaneous! Real life was welling up from the deep place inside.

Finding God the Father through Creativity

I began to experience something of the song we had sung during my very first visit to Ellel Grange, on the ten-day Healing Retreat, "The Lord your God delights in you, and in His love will give you new life." As a parent enjoys their children enjoying themselves, God was delighting in me enjoying myself! I had never been able to call Him Father. The word had always stuck in my throat, but something was beginning to change.

One day I had made some cards, and as I turned round I knocked a glass of water all over them. I was so disappointed that they were spoilt, but as I felt the disappointment, I knew that God was disappointed too, not for the sake of the cards that were ruined, but I knew He was sad because of all I had put into them of myself. Suddenly I wasn't worried about the cards anymore, but overwhelmed that God cared that much about me!

Later when the cards had dried out, I cut away the parts that had been damaged and remounted them on new backgrounds, and was surprised to find that they looked much better than the originals. Again, God used this to speak to me about what He was doing in my life. The dictionary states that "to restore" means "to bring back to a former or original condition," but God was showing me that when He restores, He multiplies and gives back even more. I knew this was biblically true, from the story of Job whom God restored and gave back twice as much as he had before he lost virtually everything (Job 42:10-12).

And God spoke even more profoundly to me one evening when I had again decided to make a card for someone. I was looking around for something to use to make the card and spotted an empty chocolate box in the bin. It had a picture of a rose on it, which I knew would be perfect, if I cut it out and mounted it on a nice background.

As I plucked the scrunched-up box from the bin and carefully cut out the rose, God reminded me that when I was in the psychiatric hospital, I had felt as if I was a piece of rubbish in the waste bin. But He had seen me not as rubbish but as a beautiful rose, and He had rescued me. He was stripping away the dross and restoring me at the core, so that He would ultimately be able to draw together all the broken parts, and I would be healed and whole and able to live my life, giving glory back to Him.

I thought about the fragrance of a rose and marveled that maybe one day I might have the privilege of bringing the fragrance of Jesus to others who needed Him (2 Corinthians 2:15).

Lost and Found

Through relationship and through creativity, God was drawing out and nurturing the "real me," the inner child that I had lost. He was pouring hope into this immature, hopeless place. I remember looking into Fiona's eyes and I knew she could see the "real me," and from that innermost place I said to her, "You *know* me, don't you?" "Yes," she said tenderly, "I know you." It meant such a lot, not to be hidden and overridden, but to be known and accepted.

But it wasn't just Fiona who knew me. God knew me. It was Him who was working through Fiona and Anna to find me. Psalm 139 begins, "O Lord, you have searched me and you know me," and goes on to say that we can never be lost to God. All the years I had lived in the "adult place" with the core of my identity lost to me, I had never been lost to God, and now He was doing His work of restoring the pearl that He had found.

The Family of God in Action

For the first three years of my visits to Ellel Grange, I never left the confines of the small counseling flat, except to get into the car to go home. The only people I ever saw and related with there were the small group of counselors who were working with me. There were many more members of the Ellel Grange team, with whom I was too afraid to come into contact.

However, as God was reaching in and strengthening me, I began to grow in confidence and, instead of spending mealtimes in the flat with the counseling team, I began to go with them to the Team Room in the main building so that we could eat our meals with the wider team. This was a huge step for me, and an important one.

Although, to begin with, I was extremely nervous and fearful, each person I came into contact with was obviously sincerely pleased to see me. They would always have a kind word for me. They would tell me they had been praying for me and give me cards with encouraging verses from the Bible written on them, and little gifts that I knew were given with real love.

I remember one team member, as she set eyes on me for the first time, smiling broadly and flinging her arms around me, and saying, "Is this the Sarah I've been praying for all this time?" I was taken aback, and amazed that these people, who didn't really know me, genuinely cared for me.

There was an infrastructure in their lives which gave them a consistency in the way they cared. Right from the beginning, whenever I had arrived at Ellel Grange, there were always flowers and welcoming cards from the team waiting in my room for me. While I had been too afraid to mix with them over that three-year period and had shunned every expression of love that came towards me from my counselors, the wider team nonetheless prepared numerous meals for me and delivered them to the door of the flat. They took the dishes away after meal-times and washed them up; they took my clothes and washed and ironed them for me; they made sure I had extra blankets during my winter visits; and, although I hid in my bedroom afraid to come out and say "hello," they took turns to come and sleep in the room next door to me to make sure I was safe at night.

The Christian help that was freely offered and given to me at Ellel Grange was a true and living expression of family, which is God's heart for us all. He sees us as His children:

> Yet to all who received him, to those who believed in his name, he gave the right to become children of God...
>
> (John 1:12)

> How great is the love the Father has lavished on us, that we should be called children of God! And that is what we are!
>
> (1 John 3:1)

> "I will be a Father to you, and you will be my sons and daughters, says the Lord Almighty."
>
> (2 Corinthians 6:18)

As I was venturing across to the main building at Ellel Grange for my meals, I began to see that there were others coming for help. I began to grasp that in this place was God's family in action. It was how He intended His family to operate.

I had never understood what family really meant before, but it gave me something to build on, and ultimately gave me that sense of belonging and acceptance that deep down I had always longed for.

CHAPTER 11

Don't Leave Me!

As my confidence was growing, some of my fears were losing their grip, and at home there were definite signs of progress.

Instead of keeping myself hidden indoors through the debilitating fear of people that had gripped me for so long, I started to venture out into the garden again. This was something I hadn't done for years, but I began to have a desire to sow some seeds in the greenhouse, to nurture them and watch them grow. And as time went by, I was keen to dig the little plants into the garden, but I didn't want them in straight lines anymore! I wanted to be creative! I was so excited that, at last, some of those self-imposed rules were losing their grip.

I started to go for walks with John along the beach or in the countryside. And gradually I began to brave the weekly shopping trip to the supermarket. I was nervous at first, keeping my head bowed and holding onto John's arm, but I no longer escaped back to the car, and each time I went it became a little bit easier.

Going Back to Church

Even though I hadn't been to church for years, my rector, David, and his wife, Caroline, had continued to pray faithfully for me over the time I had been receiving help. Occasionally they came to visit me at home to see how I was doing.

Observing a growing strength and confidence, David asked if I felt ready to go back to church. It was a fearful prospect, but there was something in me that didn't want to be in isolation anymore and, despite the fear, I wanted to get out into life. He suggested the midweek service, because fewer people attended this than the Sunday services, and he thought this might be easier for me. I said I would go.

For the first few weeks, I arrived exactly as the service started, sat in the chair nearest the door on the end of the back row and left as David was praying the final prayer. It was the best way of avoiding having to speak to anyone. During the service I trembled in fear, and sometimes couldn't open my mouth to join in the hymns, because I knew I wouldn't be able to hold back the tears if I did. But I kept going back, and steadily the fears loosened their grip. Eventually I began to stay for a few minutes and chat tentatively to others after the service. People were sensitive and kind, and I began to relax.

Although these were my only outings and I was still locked in obsessively cleaning and tidying the house, in between my visits to Ellel Grange life was beginning to gain some sense of normality. John and I were both encouraged and thankful for the progress I was making.

Yet there was one distressing and intensely frustrating issue that stood like a massive boulder, blocking the final stretch of the road to freedom.

Relationship Addiction

From the early days of my visits to Ellel Grange, I had always had a fear of falling into an unhealthy dependency on my counselors. For a long time the emotionally needy child in me had been separate and hidden, but as God had been drawing out and nurturing me to life through Fiona and Anna, I had eventually not only bonded with them, but formed an unhealthy relationship addiction.

Neither Fiona nor Anna had ever had an unhealthy need for me. It was entirely from my side that the relationship became unbalanced. And it was devastating. I felt I had switched one addiction for another. Instead of being bulimic, self-harming and suicidal, I had a relationship addiction, and all the separation anxiety that went with it.

Separation Anxiety

During the times I was at Ellel Grange, as the moment approached for Fiona and Anna to leave to go home at night, a battle would begin to rage in me. As an adult I wanted to take control and shut the inner child down, but it became harder and harder to override the panic that rose up from inside. In the end, I couldn't control it anymore at the point that Fiona and Anna walked out of the door to go home, and I would become a hysterical mess, screaming at them, "Don't leave me! Please, don't leave me!" It didn't matter how much reassurance they offered before they left, it was always the same and, in fact, had got steadily worse.

When I was at home, I became unable to control a growing obsession with where Fiona and Anna were at any given time, who they were with and what they were doing. I was intensely jealous of their families. In reality, the jealousy was the anguished feelings I had pushed away in my childhood when, as a deprived little girl, I had seen other children with caring parents and desperately wanted to have their families instead of mine. But, as the adult me, I didn't understand this. I just hated being jealous.

From deep down inside, I longed for contact with Fiona and Anna day and night, and whenever I was in conversation with them, whether it was at Ellel Grange or on the phone at home, I made impossible demands and childish, angry accusations at them. I projected onto them everything that, in reality, I felt about my mother: "You don't like me! ... You don't love me! ... You want to get rid of me!"

As the adult trying to live everyday life, I was like a person with an alcohol or drug dependency. I hated the way I was. It was utterly tormenting. There were times when I was coping reasonably well with life, making good steps forward, and appeared virtually "normal," and then there were other times when the cravings, the mood swings and the angry outbursts would shoot to the fore from inside and overwhelm me. Each time it took me by surprise and shocked me.

And just as any addict's behavior affects their family and those around them, so did mine. It was like being a person with a double life. John and the children never knew when I would next erupt into wildly uncontrolled, frenzied and explosive demands for Fiona or Anna's time and attention.

They Shouldn't Have Let Me Become Dependent!

Some people would say that Fiona, Anna and the team shouldn't have allowed me to become so dependent on them. For a long time I argued this point vehemently myself. However, as I struggled through the issue, I eventually conceded and yielded to owning the truth of the mess.

As a child, I had been totally deprived of love. Bonding, cherishing, gentleness, kindness, affirmation and encouragement are legitimate needs that every child has, and depriving a child of having these legitimate needs met amounts to cruelty which scars a child for life.

The withholding of all love had left me with a huge vacuum inside, a place of absolute deprivation at the core of my being. This was what Fiona and Anna had reached, and as they had reached it, as the "adult me" I had necessarily connected with it too. I had touched and felt the place in me where there was *nothing* and, because of that nothingness, that complete absence of *being* in life, there was a frenzy of panic and fear, an intense desperation for something or someone to connect to, who would affirm to me that I was a person, to feed me with the love I needed, to draw me out of nothingness and into life. In this destitute place in me, it was nothing less than a matter of survival, and the desperate question: can I exist?

Such was the intensity of emotion and fear inside that I was totally incapable of controlling it using my mind, other than "chopping and blocking" it, cutting it off from my conscious thinking. But that had never made it cease to exist. It had simply buried the desperate need, the desperate need that was me, the inner child.

And this inner child in me longed for bonding and the tender mother-love God intends every child to have, so that I could develop emotionally and gain a full and rounded, true sense of personal worth and security. This inner child was desperate to be noticed, to be wanted, needed, significant and special.

Not only had my parents emotionally abandoned me, and my God-given needs never been met, but I had abandoned me too. I had pushed the immature part underground with its excruciating deprivation, pain and raging sense of injustice. And I had never let it have expression. This is why there was such a raging sense of injustice inside. As the "adult me," I believed this to be bad and wrong, in order to deal with it.

God had been drawing out and nurturing the abandoned part to life through Fiona and Anna. They had accepted the little girl, encouraged her and met that aching need to be loved. They had also received *her* love, something my parents had never done, and this had helped me to grow in my own sense of worth and value.

There was no doubt that God had used them powerfully in demonstrating what love is. I couldn't have grasped it if they had sat the other side of a desk and told me I didn't need to be upset that my parents didn't love me, because God loves me.

I believe wholeheartedly that God's unconditional love is the only true remedy for the abused, the unloved, the broken-hearted, but how can a person know what that love is if it is never demonstrated to them through human channels?

Attachment Disorder

Although I didn't understand it, the problem was that I was attaching my pain to Fiona and Anna. I was effectively saying to them, "You've found this child in me. You've bonded with her. You take responsibility for her when she starts screaming for attention." Why? Because I was afraid of the pain and I didn't believe that God alone could meet my need.

I wouldn't allow myself to feel pain if Fiona and Anna weren't there to comfort me. Whenever they had finally closed the door behind them and driven off in their cars, or I had driven off to go home, as soon as I could I forcefully shut down the inner child and all the need, and overrode it.

It was no wonder the child in me longed to be with them. When I was at home I was back to being an automaton, a robot obsessively cleaning and tidying, and shutting this very real part of me back in a prison.

A Fantasy World

From the inside, it was as if I had been a drowning child, and Fiona and Anna were a life raft that had finally come along to rescue me. I had reached out and clung to them, literally for dear life. At home, imprisoned and silenced again, there was an utter desperation to keep reaching out for them, because it was only when I was with them that I was given the freedom to "be in life" and to express myself.

Out of desperation, the child in me formed an illusion around Fiona and Anna. Never having been loved by my own mother, I saw them as perfect mother figures. They were kind and gentle, patient and loving. They had all the attributes my own mother had lacked and, subconsciously, I was saying to myself, "This is what I always wanted – a mother to look after me, to fix me, to comfort me, to make me feel special." Subconsciously, I transposed my aching inner need on to them to comfort me and make me feel special.

Without cognitive recognition of what I was doing, I chopped and blocked out the reality that they had their own lives and families, believing instead that they could meet my need for a mother. In the fantasy world that came out of my subconscious, I truly believed that Fiona and/or Anna could be my mother, and all my problems would be solved.

In the end, in my illusion, Fiona became an image rather than who she is in reality, and I was using this image in an attempt to fill my inner loneliness. This felt as if it worked each time I did it but, in fact, it drained me and caused me more pressure and torment. The only real hope and peace I had, was when I received and connected to the truth: the truth of my emptiness and abandonment, and the truth that I was not orphaned or abandoned by the One who created me and knew me.

Can There Be Real Freedom from Addiction?

As the adult trying to live everyday life, I was intensely angry that the child in me was so intent on trying to make Fiona and Anna be my mother. I knew it was wrong. It was bad, I didn't want to be doing it, and I hated it. I had no compassion for this needy part, only hatred. But I couldn't stop it.

Whenever I was with Fiona and Anna, I was like an alcoholic with a bottle of whisky on the table in front of me. I couldn't stop myself trying to get them to fill the emptiness inside me and meet my need. My mind would run down the track, "Everything's all right now, I'm with Fiona and Anna. They love me. They'll look after me." And knowing that as Christians we all belonged to the family of God, I would ask them manipulative questions, "Am I part of your family?

Do you love me?" and demand to know, "When will I see you again?"

I struggled to believe that there ever could be real freedom from this addiction that was not only horrible for me, but extremely unpleasant for Fiona and Anna, and my family too. One of my biggest fears was that, after all the lengths everyone had gone to in supporting and helping me, I would just have to pretend I was better, because I couldn't bear to let them all feel their efforts had been in vain.

In the end, I decided that the only answer to the problem was to find a way to handle it better, and to learn to live with it. I determined to be grateful for all the help and healing I had received to date, and to separate myself completely from Fiona and Anna, and to stay away from Ellel Grange. I would be like an alcoholic who is fine as long as he stays away from alcohol.

The problem was that at home I would only have to hear Fiona's name mentioned in a conversation, or receive some literature from Ellel Ministries with her picture on it, and the uncontrollable longing would surge to the fore and I would become a hysterical mess again.

Like any other addict, time and time again I resolved that I wouldn't go down that track again. But over and over again, I did.

Facing the Truth of the Loss in my Life

Hard as it was for them, neither John nor Fiona and the rest of the team ever doubted that there was a way through this to real freedom for me.

As my counselors sought God and His way forward, He began to reveal that I needed to fully own and embrace the inner child that I hated so much, not as a separate part of me, but as an integral part of my personhood. In reality, this underdeveloped place in me wasn't separate (like my fragmented parts), and wasn't "bad." I was simply using my mind to push away the very real and legitimate need for love that had never been met as it should have been in my childhood. I was pushing away what I didn't like about myself and didn't want, because it was painful.

God wasn't asking my counselors to meet that need. In reality, they couldn't. They could never be my mother, no matter how much I wanted them to. He was showing them that He wasn't going to replace what I never had. He wasn't going to change my past. He is a God of truth and reality, and He was saying it was time for me to embrace in the fullest sense the truth that I had never had any mother-love, and that I desperately wanted a substitute mother. Even though God did use Fiona and Anna to put into me, through godly nurture, aspects of parental love that I needed, they weren't to be substitutes.

God wasn't condemning me. He understood the longing and was full of compassion, but He was saying it was time to bring the loss to Him and to trust Him with it.

This was hard! I didn't want to own "Bad Me" as me! I wanted to keep pushing it away. I didn't want to agree that it was *me* that was trying to use Fiona and Anna to get my own needs met. In truth, I didn't want to own and feel the deepest pain of abandonment.

Fiona and Anna knew they had reached and tended this wound, and the time had come to leave me to face feeling the need, and in feeling the need, get the fullest sense of cognizance that, "It's impossible for them to meet the need." God had done a deep work of healing in other areas of my life as an abandoned child. It was now safe and right for me to face the deepest cry.

Other than turning to alcohol or drugs to numb the intense emotional pain, I eventually saw that there wasn't any other way. And so I began to ask God to help me to face and embrace the truth of my inner unmet need and the illusion that not "Bad Me" but *I* had clung to, in a vain attempt to get my need met.

Stirring up the Nest

Deuteronomy 32:10 says,

> In a desert land he found him, in a barren and howling waste. He
> shielded him and cared for him; he guarded him as the apple of
> his eye.

God had worked through Fiona and Anna to find the needy
part of me and, for a season, to shield, care for and nurture my
"inner child," to woo to life the core that had been so utterly
crushed. But now it was the season for me to move on.

The next verse in Deuteronomy talks about God being
"like an eagle that stirs up its nest," an eagle whose young are
old enough to fly, but are reluctant to leave the comfort of the
soft, downy-lined nest. So she "stirs up the nest," removing the
soft, warm lining, so that the nest becomes uncomfortable and
the young no longer want to stay there. In a sense, she pushes
them out so that they can, ultimately, fulfill their destiny, soar-
ing on outstretched wings (Isaiah 40:31).

This was what God was asking Fiona and Anna to do. If
they had continued to nurture the inner child, I wouldn't have
been able to resist the urge to keep using their love and kindness to comfort my pain. Like the eaglets, I wouldn't have
moved out of my comfort zone, which would have led to
further intense frustration, because I could never have experienced real freedom.

Firm Boundaries

In order to "stir up the nest" and help me to walk out of the
illusion and the addictive lifestyle, the counseling team put very
necessary firm boundaries in place. Fiona and Anna did not
withdraw completely, because God was using their kind, moth-
erly natures to maintain the connection in me to my unmet
need for mother love. (The danger if they had withdrawn was

that I could have shut this down and gone back to functioning like a machine, simply trying to please others again.)

So they continued with me, but were joined by other counselors, Ian and Val, who were new to me, and whom I did not see as parental figures. There was a new proviso that I would only be seen either by Fiona or Anna on each of my visits to Lancaster, and whoever it was, would be accompanied by one of the new counselors.

My visits to Ellel Grange were cut down dramatically, and the duration of each visit to two days. And in between visits, I could contact either Ian or Val.

When the boundaries were put in place, at first I felt a deep sense of relief that these people weren't giving up on me. My relationship addiction was out in the open, and they still believed there was a pathway to real freedom. And despite all my angry, irrational outbursts, they were still willing to do whatever they could to support me, albeit in a different way from hereon in, and they had faith in God and me that there was a way through this even if it was scary. I knew I didn't deserve this and I was deeply grateful.

However, as the reality unfolded, this became both the worst and best time of my journey. It was the worst time, because although I most definitely hadn't been abandoned, I *felt* intensely abandoned. And it was the best time, because it was the key to the final breakthrough to real freedom.

Testing the Boundaries

After the boundaries had been established, the illusion wasn't instantly smashed, and the addiction didn't easily fall away.

During subsequent counseling appointments, from inside I continued to try to use Fiona and Anna to comfort my pain. But when I asked a question like, "Am I special?" they became more direct in their reply. They would say something like, "Yes, you are special, and so are Ian and Val and John and Tom and

Beth." In this way, they were refusing to feed my addiction for something false and, at the same time, focusing me on taking my real need to God, as the One who had brought my healing so far and would bring the ultimate comfort and healing.

At one level, I found this intensely difficult. I felt angry, rejected and hurt. They were no longer telling me, "God's sent us to help you. We love you. You're special to us." They had already shown me these things, but I hadn't wanted to receive this truth, believing that if I did I would lose them. Now I wanted to push them away. If they weren't going to be everything to me, I didn't want them to be anything!

They urged me on, "One day, you'll be able to choose whether you would like to spend time with us or not. You won't be demanding 'all or nothing.' We'll just be friends – normal friends." I longed for that, but I couldn't imagine how it could ever be.

Despite my angry responses, deep down I was so grateful that the team were not allowing me to manipulate them, or giving me the answers I wanted to hear. As always, they weren't giving me what I *wanted*, but what I *needed*.

Whichever counselors I saw, they were never afraid to confront me with my irrational thinking, and always did so in a kind, honest and fair way. "Sarah," they would say, "look at what you're doing. This is the pain you don't want to touch, and you're still trying to push it away." Instantly, I would be angry with them and myself, and try to push it all away again, but they would say, "Don't push it away. This is real. This is you. Let God come to you in this place of pain."

The Bible says,

> No discipline seems pleasant at the time, but painful. Later on, however, it produces a harvest of righteousness and peace for those who have been trained by it.
>
> (Hebrews 12:11)

This was my experience. It was, ultimately, those times of loving correction, that I found very hard at the time, that helped me most.

Taking Responsibility for the Child Within

Fiona and Anna knew they had put the love in that was so necessary to meet the real need in me, and because of this they were able to stand firm in refusing to take responsibility for the false need (for a substitute mother). They refused to feed the illusion I had subconsciously created. And, as they did so, I entered into the battle to take rightful responsibility myself for the child within.

I was walking towards facing my true pain, not the pain of being denied the false comfort I wanted, but the true pain of total emotional abandonment in childhood, the pain that I had never received the care and comfort I should have had from my mother when I was being brutally abused by my father.

I had tried to kill the truth of the full effect of my parents' cruelty on me. I had tried to separate from it and to override it. I had built up an illusion and sought false comfort. These had all been my ways of dealing with the problem, but none of them had been the answer. Proverbs 14:12 and 16:25 say,

> There is a way that seems right to a man, but in the end it leads to death.

This was true. The way that had seemed right to me hadn't led to freedom and the ability to enter into life at all. There was nowhere else to turn, but God was patiently wooing me to Him and His way. This is how I described the struggle in my journal (italicized sections are the "inner child" speaking):

> *From inside, I cry out, I grab, I want that, I want what others have got. It doesn't matter what it is – their house, their job, their relationships, their gifts – I want it – snatch,*

snatch, snatch! ... You wicked inner being! God says, "You're wicked and deceitful above all things!" And you *are*! Shut up! Be good! Be kind! Look good!

I want love! I want love! I want love! Snatch! Grab!

OK, I'll listen. I'll try to be kind to you. I'll give you two minutes. I'll soften my voice. What is it you want?

I want to feel my Mum's touch. I want to touch her. I want to feel her hair. I want to touch her face. Don't slam me down. Please just listen to me. Let me be who I am, how I am.

Oh, Jesus, this is me. This is the truth of my inner being. I grab and grab. I don't think I really love. I just want *their* love. I want *their* touch. I'm looking for someone to make it all OK, make it all better. I'm so sorry, Jesus. A job, a position, a place in another's affections, someone to blame, some compensation, some way to balance it all out and make it make sense, make it even, make it OK.

And You stand here – waiting – waiting – to hear the inner truth, the pain, the anger, the reality ... of me.

Jesus, I'm so sorry. Please help me to come as I truly am – to You. I don't shock You. You don't hate me. You don't disapprove. You don't condemn. You have the fullness of richness of love and acceptance, mercy, arms open wide for me – the one who hungers and grabs at other people's love, who is angry and bitter and wants to lash out and punish and make someone pay, who is jealous and resentful and seething. It's all so ugly.

But on the outside the sin is worse. I try to cover it all over, and make it all nice, pretend, pretend, perform, perform. And You don't like it, not because You are disgusted by me, but because I block *You* from coming to *me* with Your love, Your healing, protection, comfort and compassion.

Lord, I can't change this self-protective, self-preserving, self-hating and punishing nature. Lord, *You* are all-powerful – *You* can work this change in me. Please come and smash this pride. Give me humility to be who I really am – the inner person – and to come to You and receive the love I need.

This was my heart cry.

Fear of Being Alone with my Pain

This was the valley God had shown me that I needed to walk through on my own with Him, when He had given me His promise that I would "come up from the wilderness leaning on Him" (Song of Songs 8:5).

I was intensely afraid of being alone with my pain. I had been alone with a lot of pain as a child, but I was learning that if I couldn't be alone with God in pain as an adult, I would never experience the freedom and fullness of healing He wanted to bring in my life.

Learning a New Way

Whenever I had felt the craving for love and the aching for Fiona and Anna to comfort me I had habitually either hastily overridden and shut it down, or gone the other way and hysterically demanded contact with them. But, gradually, I became aware of the Holy Spirit in me leading and enabling me to respond differently. I began to realize I wasn't abandoned and alone as I had thought. God was with me, helping me to own the truth of who and how I was. I would pray something like:

Lord, this is how I am:
I wanted love as a child, and I still want love.
I want it in a way a little child wants it.
I want to go back and have it all again, but differently, the way it should have been.

And because of that, I'm trying to make Fiona and Anna be what they can't be.

This is what I do.

This is what I'm like.

I need Your help.

I can't change it.

I can't stop myself inside, from wanting my "fix-it."

But, Lord, I'm really trusting myself to You.

Please, God, help me to change.

Will You help me to allow You to do Your work in me so that You can bring the change, and I will no longer be crying out for my own "fix-it?"

It wasn't easy, and there were many times when I did go back to separating from the place of need in me, and then, when I was suddenly overwhelmed by the craving for comfort again, I was genuinely confused.

At those times, I would speak to Val, and she would help me to understand what I had done by asking something like, "Have you disconnected from your inner self? Have you pushed away the feelings?" And then I would go back to God again with a similar prayer.

I sometimes took two steps forward and one back and I often wanted to give up. But although I couldn't see it at the time, things were changing. Instead of finding my security either in overriding my need and trying to be "perfect," or in driven attachments to Fiona and Anna, I was slowly coming to terms with the truth about myself and who I really am.

I was facing the reality that there are areas of weakness, pain and sin within me that aren't separate, but part and parcel of me as a whole person. And I was learning to look to God for His comfort when I was feeling my pain and need.

CHAPTER 12

Relationship and Intimacy

God was at work in me. Instead of rejecting, hating and punishing myself, I was learning to accept myself, and this included accepting my past as part of who I am. These were major steps forward and had a very positive outworking in daily life.

Hysterical demands for Fiona and Anna became less and less frequent, and because I was no longer locked into trying to override pain and present a false image, my obsession with housework became less urgent. I began to be able to make eye contact with the checkout assistants at the supermarket and to chat more easily with people at church.

This was good fruit, and when I went back to Ellel Grange, we began to look at ways I could build on this.

Venturing Further Afield

Ellel Ministries has four centers in the UK, one of them, Glyndley Manor, being on the south coast, which is much nearer to my home. Fiona suggested that I consider attending the Modular School there. This would be a series of ten weekend courses over a period of a year, and the same group of people would attend each weekend. The teaching would be useful to me, but more importantly it would give me the opportunity to build relationships with others.

At first, I was vehemently opposed to the idea. The old fear of people instantly surged to the fore: What would people think of me? How could I introduce myself? I couldn't say, "I'm Sarah, I'm a teacher or a nurse or a counselor..." because I wasn't! And what if everyone else could say something like that?

I struggled, but eventually, knowing this was the next step God was leading me to take, I booked onto the school. I asked if I could have a bedroom to myself each weekend. The course host said she would do her best but it might not always be possible.

This worried me, and so did the thought of the inevitable introductions there would be on the first evening of the first weekend. I wanted to be able to just say, "I'm Sarah," without wishing I could hide behind a profession. I knew I wouldn't be able to do that; I knew I would feel nervous and my cheeks would burn, which in turn would embarrass me more, but I prayed that by the end of the year I would have reached the place where I really would be comfortable just being me.

Each month as I set off for Glyndley Manor, I prayed urgently that there would be a single room waiting for me. To my relief there was, and at every opportunity in between teaching sessions I would slip back to its solitude and safety.

But between the third and fourth weekends, God reminded me that the main reason I was undertaking this series of courses was to take steps out of isolation. I knew I had to make some choices that went against my natural inclinations. So I amended my booking for the next weekend course, requesting accommodation in a multiple occupancy room.

I arrived early hoping to be first, so that I wouldn't have to walk into a room full of people already there, and in the hope that I would be able to choose the bed that was furthest away from the others. As I walked into the room I was booked into, I saw it had five beds. Immediately, it reminded me of being back at the ward in the psychiatric hospital. My heart was beating fast, but as the other women arrived I tried to hide my fear, and as they began to chatter, I relaxed. They were nice people, and little by little I joined in their conversations.

As we progressed through the school, it became obvious that we were all on a journey. Some people shared a lot about the issues they struggled with in their lives, and others shared very little. Either way it was fine, and I found I didn't have to explain myself to anyone. God was giving me new opportunities to learn to "just be me."

I stopped escaping to the bedroom at coffee breaks and joined the other guests, either in the lounge or going for walks around the lovely grounds. Eventually I realized I had turned a hundred-and-eighty degrees when, instead of feeling relieved when it was time to go home, I began to feel sad at saying "bye-bye" to my newfound friends.

A Family Holiday

During the time I was working through the Modular School, with almost no warning John was suddenly made redundant from his job, having worked at the same company for over thirty years. It came as a big shock, which left him reeling. By this time, Tom was nineteen and at university, though still living at home, and Beth was seventeen and just about to leave home to go to university.

John began to take stock of all that we had been through as a family over the previous eight years. As he reflected on the fact that the children were no longer children, and there was every possibility they may not be living at home for much longer, he had a desire to use his redundancy money to book a once-in-a-lifetime family holiday. He had always wanted to go to Australia. Tom and Beth were keen to go too, so he asked me if I thought I could manage this big trip. It would be a major undertaking for me, but I prayed about it and, despite my fears, I knew it was right to say "yes."

We were away for three and a half weeks and, during this time, the vulnerable place of need in me was hidden away inside. There were times when I was nervous, but I didn't have any of the immature, childlike responses, the cravings for love or the panics, that had previously come from the "child within."

Partly, I believe this was because I was now owning this insecure place in me, and no longer batting it down. It was no longer imprisoned and cut off, but there was a connection to life in the outside world from within. The fact that I was able to undertake this holiday was the fruit of all the strength God had been imparting into the inner place, that was now coming through to the "outer adult me."

I believe that God, in His mercy, also kept safe the "inner place" where there was still deep shame and mistrust, just as He was keeping safe all the fragmented parts, so that as a family we could have this extremely precious time together.

For most of Tom and Beth's lives, I had been dysfunctional, and they had grown up tiptoeing round my problems. It was a miracle that they hadn't rebelled and gone off the rails and turned against me. I can only believe that it was God's hand on us, and John's steadfastness, that kept us all together through such turbulent times, to the point that we were able to have a major holiday together as a family unit. John, Tom and Beth didn't have to feel they were taking a semi-functional wife and mother with them. Instead it was a very special and important time, to all intents and purposes as a "normal family."

We now have treasured memories of swimming at the Great Barrier Reef and seeing the amazing coral and tropical fish, and of getting up incredibly early one morning to watch the sun rise over Ayers' Rock, and on another occasion climbing up one of the towers on the Sydney Harbour Bridge and seeing the amazing vista below us. We are so thankful that, notwithstanding the hard times, we are able to look back and remember some really good times as a family.

The Issue of Intimacy

When we originally booked the holiday my biggest fear was the sleeping arrangements. We asked for a twin-bedded room for John and me at each location. In the lead-up to the time before we left, my instinct was to ring and check, and double-check, that at each hotel there would be a twin, and not a double room, waiting for us, but I knew God was going to use this time to help me address the issue of intimacy with John. So, instead of making phone calls to the travel agent, I told God that if it turned out that there was a double room at any of the locations, I would sleep in it with John.

Three out of the four hotels had double beds in the rooms reserved for us. As soon as I saw them, I was full of fear, but knowing I needed to keep my word, trust God and honor John, I didn't go back on my promise. To begin with I slept all night, gripping the side of the bed, almost falling off the edge. John was unbelievably patient with me, and little by little I relaxed.

When we returned home after nearly a month away, I knew in my heart that it wouldn't be right to go back to sleeping in my old bedroom alone again, so I moved back into our room. It wasn't what I wanted in my feelings. In my feelings I was afraid of intimacy. I couldn't even say the word "sex." It felt so wrong and so dirty. But I knew I couldn't make decisions based on my feelings. I had to trust that if I did what I knew God was speaking into my heart, and if I honored John, that my feelings would ultimately come into line.

I can truthfully say that over time, as I have made good choices, and through John's patience, understanding and love for me, God has done what I once thought was utterly impossible. He has taken away my fear of intimacy, my feelings and attitude that were once so defiled have become normal and healthy, and I am completely free in the area of my sexuality.

CHAPTER 13

In the Hands of My Father

I had climbed a mountain with God, with John and with my counselors, as I had walked the path to freedom from mental illness. And I always thought that when I reached the summit I would have a new perspective – God's perspective – in place of all my old beliefs and the guilt, fear and insecurity that had kept me in the depths. But I discovered along the way that, much as I was focused on the end product of "healing," God was interested in the journey itself, and what He was doing along the way.

He had not only revealed hidden parts of me and shown me who I am, but He had revealed His own nature and character and shown me who He is, too.

Through John and the children, and Fiona and Anna and the rest of the team, He had shown me what His unconditional love was like: it was gracious and merciful towards me. It was patient, kind, tender, forgiving and persevering. His heart was completely *for* the absolute best for me. And with His love, He had rebuilt my shattered trust so that I could, ultimately, believe in His love and receive it in my heart.

Where Is my Security?

There were props I had clung to on the way up the mountain, and there were supports He had given me as I had needed them. There were hopes and dreams I had found for the

future, including a desire to help others who come from similar backgrounds.

But God was leading me to a time and place where He
would ask me to forsake everything else I clung to for security
and, looking for no other guarantees, to jump off the mountain into His arms. This had never been in my thinking! But
He showed me that even the walk to healing itself, had given
me a sense of security, and He wanted me to let go of it.

This came as a shock to me. It felt as if God was being
cruel, and I wrestled with this for a long time. Eventually, I
found this verse in the Bible:

> for love is as strong as death,
> its jealousy unyielding as the grave.
> It burns like blazing fire, like a mighty flame.
>
> (Song of Songs 8:6)

I began to understand two things: firstly, God loves every one
of us so much that He is jealous for first place in our lives and,
secondly, He wants us to know the freedom and peace of not
having to cling to anything else, simply our trust in Him.

I felt as if I was standing at the edge of a precipice, wanting to be utterly dependent on Him, to allow Him to be my
all-sufficient Father, wanting to trust that His everlasting arms
were going to catch me when I jumped. But each time I took
a deep breath and said, "OK, Lord, I'm going to trust You with
everything," unanswered questions would flood into my mind:
"If I do this, will it mean I will never go back to Ellel Grange...
never again see the people I've grown to love?", "Will I never
have another counseling appointment?", "Will I need to get a
job?", "What will life be like?", "What about the pain and anger
I'm still carrying?" As fear overwhelmed me, I would suddenly
step back from the edge.

I struggled hugely to relinquish my supports, including
the compulsions I still clung to, which somehow made me feel
secure, and to let go finally of the very depth of pain in my

life and trust it to God. God was asking me to release every-thing to Him and to rest simply in *being* who He had shown me I am, *His* child with my own unique identity, likes and dis-likes, strengths and weaknesses, joys and pains... and to rest in His love.

God didn't ask me, and wouldn't have asked me, to freely jump into His arms when I began the journey at the bottom of the mountain. He had waited until He had rebuilt what had been smashed and stolen from me. He had gently and patiently led me to this point, and then He waited. Yet still, in my humanity, I protested at what seemed too much for Him to ask.

I was like a butterfly in a chrysalis. The new life was beck-oning me, and I was struggling to emerge from the old, that for a time had been my safety and security. Yet in the struggle, just as the butterfly's wings are strengthened to fly, so I was growing in trust.

Jumping into the Everlasting Arms

In July 2006, during a visit to Ellel Grange, God's Holy Spirit had brought me to the place where I was finally ready to release the pain, injustice and anger that for so long had been locked in the "little girl" in me. I didn't want to separate out and hold anything back anymore. I wanted to come to God with *all* that I am.

I went outside with a huge sheet of paper and some large pots of paints and, kneeling on the lawn, it was as if I could see the cross in front of me. Fully owning, embracing and feeling my deepest emotions, I covered my hands in paint and began to shout out the feelings: bitter, resentful, angry, hateful, mur-derous and vengeful feelings. With each shout I slammed one hand or the other, and sometimes both hands, dripping with grey-green-black murky paint down on the paper. With tears rolling down my cheeks, the momentum grew and grew.

I was finally expressing the darkest and worst of my emotions that I had held back till now, the last vestiges of what had once seemed like a bottomless pit of negative emotion. It was like the sludge at the bottom of a bucket.

By the time I had finished there was a black, wet, slimy mess on the piece of paper, on the grass and splashed all over me, too. I knew this was representative of all the mess that had been inside me but, through the enabling power of the Holy Spirit in me, I had finally bottomed it out and laid it all to rest at the foot of the cross.

I felt a huge sense of relief and gratitude to God for sending Jesus so that I could do this. And I felt peaceful in the full assurance that as I went home after this visit, *God* was going to fill the empty place inside with His love.

Finally I had reached the place where I wasn't pretending, and I wasn't looking to someone else to meet my need. I had jumped off that mountain, trusting in His love to fill the vacuum inside that had always felt as if it could never be satisfied.

Resting in the Everlasting Arms

When I went home the next day, I wanted to get straight back into the habit of keeping busy, but God was asking me to stop "doing" and to "be," to spend time with Him, to rest and find things I *liked* to do rather than things I felt I *should* do.

It was summertime, so I spent a lot of time sitting in the garden, resting, reading and cross-stitching. I had to stand against the feelings of being selfish and lazy, the false guilt that rose up in me. But God was teaching me, "You're not a machine! It's OK to be Sarah, and to enjoy being Sarah!"

By the end of the summer, for the first time in my life, I was truly enjoying resting and just "being." In fact, it was a huge relief after a lifetime of striving that had become so much a part of my identity. I realized what a strain it had been to keep hidden the things I hadn't wanted to face, and how releasing it was to trust them to God.

God was bringing healthy balance to my life. At last, I was entering into just being me, His child, resting in His arms.

God Joins My Fragmented Parts

Three months later, during my next visit to Ellel Grange, the joining of my fragmented parts finally took place. I had always been fearful about how it would happen, what would be expected of me, and what I would be like when I was one whole person. But I had experienced such a sense of relief in embracing the "little girl" in the "adult me" that I was ready to embrace all my fragmented parts as well. God (and my counselors) had been incredibly gracious in patiently waiting for the time when I, eventually, *wanted* to be a whole person.

I didn't know how God was going to do it. All I knew was that I couldn't do it myself, and I would have to be totally reliant on Him. The team prayed, asking God to do His work of growing up each of my fragmented parts and uniting me as one whole person.

I could sense Him reassuring me, gently repeating over and over again the words of 1 John 4:18, "Perfect love drives out fear." As I took this in, my natural fears were calmed and I felt relief and a sense of real peace. It was a strangely quiet time, since it was the culmination of a monumental ten-year journey from near-death to fullness of life.

The younger parts were joined together first, and finally these younger ones were joined to Sarah 18. Although, as the "adult me," I couldn't physically see Sarah 18, my eyes were closed and I could see her in my mind's eye. It was as if we were both standing facing one another with deep care for one another and smiling tentatively. We both knew without any doubt that God's Holy Spirit was right there with us. We held out our arms to embrace one another, and as we stepped close and held one another, the Holy Spirit merged us together and we became one.

I felt an instant solidity I had never felt before. Fiona prayed the words of Matthew 19:6, "What You have joined together, Lord, let man not separate," and into my mind came God's words "strong and safe."

Now all my broken parts were one, and I was "strong and safe." I knew I would never be broken again.

At first, in the quietness, my thoughts centered on the enormity of what God had done through a final simple prayer, in a matter of a few minutes. He had done something no one else could do. Years ago Dr Searle had attested to this. How could the torn and scattered petals of a rosebud, let alone a human life, ever be so restored and then reconstructed to form the strong, velvety textured, full and fragrant bloom it was originally destined to be? This is what God had done in my life.

As the hours went by, I began to sense more and more of the fullness of all the love God had poured into each part of me, now united as one. For the first time ever, I had the full memory of my life, and it began to overwhelm me. I had imagined in the past that when the time came that I could remember everything it would be the fullness of the horrific memories of my childhood that would be hard to bear. But what overwhelmed me far and beyond anything else was how so much of the goodness and love of God had been input into my life.

Previously, I had known in each part how God had loved me through Fiona, Anna and the team, and brought so much restoration and healing in each part, but I had never been able to grasp and experience the full extent of all that God had poured into me – not eight people – but just one person. I was overwhelmed by His love and goodness to me.

In Ephesians 3:16-19, Paul prays that,

> out of his glorious riches he may strengthen you with power through his Spirit in your inner being ... And I pray that you,

being rooted and established in love, may have power ... to grasp how wide and long and high and deep is the love of Christ, and to know this love that surpasses knowledge...

This prayer had been answered in my life.

Reality was the Goal

I realized then that healing had never been about attaining something, about being all "fixed" and having everything perfect! Conversely, it hadn't been about resignation to the past either, with an attitude of "I'll just have to live with it and make the best of it." I had gone through times of fearing both of these extremes.

I now knew that the goal of healing was coming to peace with myself, coming to a healthy, balanced place of resolution of my past, that doesn't negate that there are painful areas, and doesn't negate either the reality of the many good things God has brought into my life.

I have already said that there are times when I still feel the pain of my life. The difference is, I am not afraid of it anymore. When it is touched, my thoughts go something like this, "Yes, that was the truth of my life. I have come from a terrible background. I do have sadnesses, but I have a heavenly Father who has rescued me, who loves me more than any earthly parent ever could." And I thank Him for what He's done, and how He's changing me and bringing His redemption into my life. God is in the pain with me and I can draw on His comfort. He has become my true source of security. And because of that, instead of being weighed down by the consequences of my past, I am able to be outward looking for the blessings of the present and the future.

Knowing God as Father

For so long I hated the word "father." I couldn't say it because it had so many fearful connotations. The word just stuck in my throat.

Romans 8:15 says,

> For you did not receive a spirit that makes you a slave again to fear, but you received the Spirit of sonship. And by him, we cry, "Abba, Father." The Spirit himself testifies with our spirit that we are God's children.

This is my experience. Often, when I am on my own, the words "Father! Father!" just bubble up spontaneously from within me, and I know my heavenly Father is right there with me. It is so precious. Feeling as if I have truly been parented by God (albeit through human channels) and knowing Him as my unconditionally loving, heavenly Father is a joy beyond compare.

I had wanted a set of rules to obey, and to begin with I had responded to God's rules, but in the end I responded to His love. All the hate in my life has been exchanged for love, love for my heavenly Father God, love for others and a rightful love for myself.

New Life

After the joining of my fragmented parts, I had anticipated that I would need, at least, a follow-up counseling appointment at Ellel Grange, but I have never felt the need for another appointment, and nor have my counselors.

After completing a year of the Modular School at Glyndley Manor, I signed up for the second part of the School which took another year. Since then, after a year out, I have become involved in teaching and ministering to others from time to time at the different Ellel centers.

I can truthfully say that my life is completely different today. I am so grateful that I now have an inner security and strength that comes from having allowed God into my deepest place of pain. The fears that once crippled me have gone, and I have been free of all psychiatric medication for over ten years.

To help with the writing of this book, I made an appointment to see Dr Searle with John in May 2009. This was the first time we had seen him since he had discharged me twelve years previously. This is what he wrote in a letter to my GP following the appointment:

> *Sarah is now very well, I am glad to say, and she has made a fantastic recovery from her serious problems. I am sure a lot of this is down to her own faith and her own diligent efforts – supported by her husband and the therapy organization she went to see.*

For the last two years, I have been working part-time, employed by the same company as John. Two or three days a week we get in the car and go off to work together! For us, this is precious normality!

Life in the home is normal too! Recently, Tom and Beth (who have both graduated from university and are both now living and working in London) were home for the weekend.

On the Sunday afternoon they both appeared in the kitchen with John to help as I prepared a roast dinner. As the vegetables were peeled, a skewer was pressed into the chicken to test the juices and pastry for a Bakewell tart was rolled out, amidst the light-hearted conversation I felt a huge wave of gratitude well up from inside myself. This was the normality which for so long we had all longed for.

For years, I had cried out in desperation time and time again, "I want to be normal!", though I didn't really know what "normal" meant. But this was it. No one was striving to make everything perfect to keep Mum on an even keel. No one was tiptoeing round the problem of my fragility and the debilitating way it affected us as a family – the "elephant" that had stood in the room for so long. There was no elephant, and there were no tensions. We were all relaxed and simply enjoying preparing a meal together.

The cutlery didn't have to be laid out in straight lines in measured distances from the edges of the table. It didn't matter if some of the vegetable peelings accidentally fell on the floor. It didn't even matter when the Bakewell tart ended up in a dish that was too small and expanded over the sides making a sticky mess on the oven floor. Everything didn't have to be perfect anymore, and we could all laugh when it wasn't.

It was one of those precious moments that come along when I recognize afresh how things are so different to the way they used to be. I was suddenly aware of how the changes that have taken place on the inside, have brought in their wake wonderful, profound change on the outside too.

The Master Craftsman's Handiwork

Finally, the rooms we always used for counseling during my visits to Ellel Grange are in a separate building to the main house. And this building was in need of restoration. It was shabby and run down, but after I had stopped receiving help there, it came to light that there was structural damage to the building and it was, in fact, in danger of falling down! It needed urgent attention.

The maintenance team had a huge job on their hands, which they undertook diligently. Not only did they complete all the major structural repairs, but they took the opportunity to completely refurbish the rooms we had once used.

After the work had been completed I was again visiting Ellel Grange, but this time to help with some teaching on a course they were running. I went to see the renovations. As I walked around and looked out of the same window I had looked out of countless times in the past at the old, familiar beech tree, my eyes filled with tears. The view outside was exactly the same as it had always been. Nothing had changed, but inside everything had changed. What had once been neglected, worn out, dingy and, as it turned out, unstable, too, was now completely transformed. It was bright, fresh, clean and new.

I recognized the analogy instantly. The world outside hadn't changed, but inside me everything had changed, and was and is still changing. Right at the end of the Bible in Revelation 21:5, God says, "I am making everything new." My life had been like a house that had never been cared for or, worse, a house that had been vandalized, but the Master Craftsman had painstakingly restored me, and even now continues to do His work in me.

I truly am in the hands of my Father.

Postscript

As I finish my story, which isn't really my story but God's story, I would like to offer a personal encouragement to you, the reader.

If you have been cruelly neglected, unloved, betrayed, orphaned or abused or, in fact, have any needs at all, and have in any way been touched by the pages of this book, please, may I recommend to you the person of Jesus? This relationship with a loving heavenly Father, through Jesus, isn't just for me, but is for you too.

God cares about the things you have suffered in your life. He wants to heal your wounds. He wants to show you how special and precious you are to Him, and how much He loves you. And His heart's desire is to take the pain and the rejection, everything that's assailed you and all the things you've done too, and He wants to give back, to restore and redeem all that's been lost. This is what He longs to do for every person who comes to Him just as they are. He is the Giver of life both here on earth and in eternity to come.

> He [God] has sent me [Jesus] to bind up the broken-hearted, to proclaim freedom for captives and release from darkness for the prisoners ... to comfort all who mourn ... to bestow on them a crown of beauty instead of ashes, the oil of gladness instead of mourning, and a garment of praise instead of a spirit of despair.
>
> (Isaiah 61:1-3)

Publisher's Note

Sarah's story is the true record of her healing.

We are grateful to Dr Searle for writing the Foreword to her book, but please note that he is unable to enter into any correspondence.

Further information about Ellel Ministries may be obtained by referring to their website at:

www.ellelministries.org

or writing to:

Ellel Ministries, Ellel Grange, Lancaster,
LA2 0HN, England. Tel: +44 (0)1524 751651

Books on Healing

Intercession & Healing
Fiona Horrobin (as featured in the book *Sarah*)
978-185240-500-7 • £7.99 • PB • 176pp

Hope & Healing for the Abused
Paul & Liz Griffin
978-185240-480-2 • £6.99 • PB •128pp

Powerful True Stories

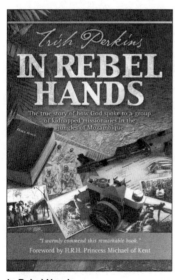

In Rebel Hands
Trish Perkins
978-185240-504-5 • £12.99 • PB • 416pp

Frida
Frida Gashumba
978-185240-475-8 • £8.99 • PB • 176pp

www.sovereignworld.com
View all our titles online or request a catalogue (+44 (0)1524 75 38 05